LAST JUDGMENT

SUPPLEMENTS

LAST JUDGMENT

SUPPLEMENTS

The Portable New Century Edition

EMANUEL SWEDENBORG

Translated from the Latin by George F. Dole
and Jonathan S. Rose

SWEDENBORG FOUNDATION
West Chester, Pennsylvania

Originally published in Latin as two separate works:
   Last Judgment: *De Ultimo Judicio, et de Babylonia Destructa: Ita Quod Omnia, Quae in Apocalypsi Praedicta Sunt, Hodie Impleta Sint: Ex Auditis et Visis* (London, 1758)
   Supplements: *Continuatio de Ultimo Judicio: Et de Mundo Spirituali* (Amsterdam, 1763)

Printed in the United States of America.

ISBN (portable)   978-0-87785-416-6
ISBN (e-book of portable edition)   978-0-87785-681-8

The text of *Last Judgment* is also included in *The Shorter Works of 1758,* ISBN 978-0-87785-482-1.
The text of *Supplements* is also included in *The Shorter Works of 1763,* ISBN 978-0-87785-503-3.

Library of Congress Cataloging-in-Publication Data

Names: Swedenborg, Emanuel, 1688–1772. | Dole, George F., translator. | Rose, Jonathan S., 1956– translator. | Swedenborg, Emanuel, 1688–1772. De ultimo judicio et Babylonia destructa. English. | Swedenborg, Emanuel, 1688–1772. Continuatio de ultimo judicio et de mundo spirituali. English.
Title: Last judgment ; Supplements : the portable new century edition / Emanuel Swedenborg ; Last judgment translated from the Latin by George F. Dole and Jonathan S. Rose ; Supplements translated from the Latin by George F. Dole.
Description: West Chester, Pennsylvania : Swedenborg Foundation, 2018. | "Originally published in Latin as two separate works: De ultimo judicio, et de Babylonia destructa: Ita quod omnia, quae in Apocalypsi praedicta sunt, hodie impleta sunt: Ex auditis et visis (London, 1758) Continuatio de ultimo judicio: Et de mundo spirituali (Amsterdam, 1763)."
Identifiers: LCCN 2014049966 | ISBN 9780877854166 (alk. paper)
Subjects: LCSH: Judgment Day—Early works to 1800. | New Jerusalem Church—Doctrines.
Classification: LCC BX8712 .L4 2018 | DDC 289/.4—dc23
LC record available at https://lccn.loc.gov/2014049966

Senior copy editor, Alicia L. Dole
Text designed by Joanna V. Hill
Ornaments from the first Latin editions, 1758 and 1763
Typesetting by Alicia L. Dole
Cover designed by Karen Connor

For information contact:
Swedenborg Foundation
320 North Church Street
West Chester, PA 19380 USA
Telephone: (610) 430-3222
Web: www.swedenborg.com
E-mail: info@swedenborg.com

Contents

Supplement on the Spiritual World

Conventions Used in This Work

L AST *Judgment* was originally published in 1758; *Supplements* appeared in 1763. *Supplements* is made up of two smaller works: one intended to augment the earlier *Last Judgment,* and a separate work intended to augment information Swedenborg had previously published on the spiritual world. It is the shared content on the topic of the Last Judgment that prompts the publication of these works in one volume.

Section numbers Following a practice common in his time, Swedenborg divided his published theological works into sections numbered in sequence from beginning to end. His original section numbers have been preserved in this edition; they appear in boxes in the outside margins. Traditionally, these sections have been referred to as "numbers" and designated by the abbreviation "n." In this edition, however, the more common section symbol (§) is used to designate the section numbers, and the sections are referred to as such.

Subsection numbers Because many sections throughout Swedenborg's works are too long for precise cross-referencing, Swedenborgian scholar John Faulkner Potts (1838–1923) further divided them into subsections; these have since become standard, though minor variations occur from one edition to another. They are indicated by bracketed numbers that appear in the text itself: [2], [3], and so on. Since the beginning of the first subsection always coincides with the beginning of the section proper, it is not labeled in the text.

Citations of Swedenborg's text As is common in Swedenborgian studies, text citations of Swedenborg's works refer not to page numbers but to section numbers, which unlike page numbers are uniform in most editions. In citations the section symbol (§) is generally omitted after the title of a work by Swedenborg. Thus "*Secrets of Heaven* 29" would refer to section 29 (§29) of Swedenborg's *Secrets of Heaven,* not to page 29 of any edition. Subsection numbers are given after a colon; a reference such as "29:2" would indicate subsection 2 of section 29. The reference "29:1" would indicate the first subsection of section 29, though that subsection is not in fact labeled in the text. Where section numbers stand alone without titles, their function is indicated by the prefixed section symbol;

for example, §29:2. However, section marks are generally omitted in Swedenborg's indexlike references to *Secrets of Heaven*.

Citations of the Bible Biblical citations in this edition follow the accepted standard: a semicolon is used between book references and between chapter references, and a comma between verse references. Therefore "Matthew 5:11, 12; 6:1; 10:41, 42; Luke 6:23, 35" would refer to Matthew chapter 5, verses 11 and 12; Matthew chapter 6, verse 1; Matthew chapter 10, verses 41 and 42; and Luke chapter 6, verses 23 and 35. Swedenborg often incorporated the numbers of verses not actually represented in his text when listing verse numbers for a passage he quoted; these apparently constitute a kind of "see also" reference to other material he felt was relevant. This edition also follows Swedenborg where he cites contiguous verses individually (for example, John 14:8, 9, 10, 11), rather than as a range (John 14:8–11). Occasionally this edition supplies a full, conventional Bible reference where Swedenborg omits one after a quotation.

Quotations in Swedenborg's works Some features of the original Latin texts have been modernized in this edition. For example, Swedenborg's first editions generally rely on context or italics rather than on quotation marks to indicate passages taken from the Bible or from his other works. The manner in which these conventions are used in the original suggests that Swedenborg did not belabor the distinction between direct quotation and paraphrase; but in this edition, directly quoted material is indicated by either block quotations or quotation marks, and paraphrased material is presented without such indicators. In passages of dialog as well, quotation marks have been introduced that were not present as such in the original. Furthermore, Swedenborg did not mark his omissions from or changes to material he quoted, a practice in which this edition generally follows him.

Italicized terms Any words in indented scriptural extracts that are here set in italics reflect a similar emphasis in the first editions.

Swedenborg's footnotes The author's footnotes, indicated by superscript letters in the main body of the text, consist of cross-references to his previously published *Secrets of Heaven* (1749–1756). It should be observed that Swedenborg's general practice was to use the lettering series *a–z, aa–zz,* and *aaa–zzz* before starting over at *a,* whereas in this edition the lettering starts over after each chapter heading.

Changes to and insertions in the text This edition is based on the text of the first Latin editions, published by Swedenborg himself. It incorporates the silent emendation of minor errors, not only in the text proper but in

Bible verse references and in section references to Swedenborg's other published theological works. The text has also been changed without notice where the verse numbering of the Latin Bible cited by Swedenborg differs from that of modern English Bibles. Throughout the translation, references or cross-references that were implied but not stated have been inserted in square brackets; for example, [Luke 21:10, 11, 25]. By contrast, references that occur in parentheses reflect references that appear in the first editions; for example, (Isaiah 51:6), (see §9 above). Square brackets are also used to indicate additions not directly reflecting wording in the first Latin editions, but necessary for the understanding of the text; this marking of expansions has been used sparingly, however, even at the risk of some inconsistency in its application.

Chapter numbering Swedenborg did not number the chapters of *Last Judgment* or *Supplements.* His decision not to do so seems to have been deliberate, and in accord with it chapter numbers are not included in the text. However, because some studies of his works make reference to chapter numbers, the table of contents provides them.

Biblical titles Swedenborg refers to the Hebrew Scriptures as the Old Testament and to the Greek Scriptures as the New Testament; his terminology has been adopted in this edition.

Further information This Portable Edition volume supplies only the translated text of these works. For introductory material on *Last Judgment* and *Supplements,* and for annotations on their subject matter, with extensive indexes, the reader is referred to the Deluxe New Century Edition volumes *The Shorter Works of 1758* and *The Shorter Works of 1763,* respectively. In general, the introductions in this series discuss the key ideas presented in each work, as well as the relationship of those ideas to the history of ideas, and specifically to their eighteenth-century context. The annotations provide definitions of unfamiliar terms; clarification of direct or indirect references to people, places, events, or other works; and information on matters that present challenges to current readers because of changes in culture over time.

Problematic content Occasionally Swedenborg makes statements that, although mild by the standards of eighteenth-century theological discourse, now read as harsh, dismissive, or insensitive. The most problematic are assertions about or criticisms of various religious traditions and their adherents—including Judaism, ancient or contemporary; Roman Catholicism; Islam; and the Protestantism in which Swedenborg himself grew up. These statements are far outweighed in size and importance by other passages in Swedenborg's works earnestly maintaining the value of every individual and of all religions. This wider context is discussed in the introductions and annotations of the Deluxe editions mentioned above. In the present format, however, problematic statements must be retained without comment. The other option—to omit them—would obscure some aspects of Swedenborg's presentation and in any case compromise its historicity.

The Last Judgment

and

Babylon Destroyed

Showing That

at This Day
All the Predictions
of the Book of Revelation
Have Been Fulfilled

Drawn from Things Heard and Seen

The Last Judgment
and
Babylon Destroyed

"Judgment Day" Does Not Mean
the End of the World

I F people have no knowledge of the Word's spiritual meaning, they cannot help but understand the Last Judgment to mean the end of everything visible to the eye in this world, since it says that at that time both
heaven and earth will pass away and that God will create a new heaven
and a new earth. They find further support for this interpretation in the
fact that it says all people will then rise from their graves and that the good
will then be separated from the evil, and so on [Matthew 25:31–46; 1 Thes-
salonians 4:15–17; Revelation 20:11–15].

That, however, is what a literal reading of the Word says, because
the literal meaning of the Word is earthly and resides on the lowest level
of the divine design (though even there absolutely everything contains
some spiritual meaning). As a result, people who understand the Word
only in its literal meaning can be led to various conclusions, as has indeed

happened throughout the Christian world—resulting in any number of heresies, for each of which people find biblical support.

[2] Still, since no one has as yet realized that there is spiritual meaning throughout the Word and in every detail, or has even realized what spiritual meaning is, people who have held this opinion of the Last Judgment are to be forgiven. However, let them now know that the heavens we see above us are not going to pass away, and neither is this earth that we are living on. No, both of them are going to survive. And let them now know that the "new heaven" and "new earth" mean a new church both in heaven and on earth. I speak of a new church in heaven since there is a church there just as there is on earth, because the Word and sermons exist in heaven as on earth and angels have a divine worship that is similar to ours. The difference, though, is that everything there is in a more perfected state because it exists in a spiritual world rather than an earthly one. So all the people there are spiritual people and not earthly, the way they were in this world. On this subject, see my book about heaven, especially where it discusses our union with heaven through the Word (*Heaven and Hell* 303–310) and deals with divine worship in heaven (*Heaven and Hell* 221–227).

2   The following are some passages in the Word where it speaks of the end of heaven and earth:

> Lift up your eyes to heaven and look on the earth beneath. The heavens will vanish away like smoke and the earth will grow old like a garment. (Isaiah 51:6)

> Behold, I am going to create new heavens and a new earth, and the former ones will not be remembered. (Isaiah 65:17)

> I will make new heavens and a new earth. (Isaiah 66:22)

> The stars of heaven fell to the earth, and heaven receded like a scroll that is rolled up. (Revelation 6:13, 14)

> I saw a great throne and the one who sat on it, from whose face earth and heaven fled away. And no place was found for them. (Revelation 20:11)

> I saw a new heaven and a new earth; the first heaven and the first earth had passed away. (Revelation 21:1)

In these passages the "new heaven" does not mean the sky that we see with our eyes but heaven itself, where humankind is gathered in. Ever since the beginning of the Christian church a heaven has been gathered from

the whole of humankind. The people in it were not angels, though, but
spirits, of various religions. This is the heaven meant by the first heaven
that would pass away. There will be further detail about their situation
in what follows [§§65–72]. I mention it here only so that the reader may
know what is meant by the first heaven that would pass away.

Anyone who thinks with any rational enlightenment can perceive that
this is not referring to the sky that has stars in it, the vast firmament of creation, but to heaven spiritually understood, where angels and spirits live.

Until now, people have not realized that "a new earth" means a new
church on earth, for the simple reason that they have thought "earth" in
the Word means earth, when in fact it means the church. In a nonspiri-
tual sense it does mean the earth, but spiritually understood it means the
church. This is because if we are focused on the spiritual meaning—that
is, if we ourselves are as spiritual as angels—when it says "earth" in the
Word we do not understand it to mean the earth itself but the people
who live on it and their worship of God. That is why "earth" means the
church (on this point see the references from *Secrets of Heaven* cited in
the footnote).[a],[*]

---

a. "Earth" in the Word means the Lord's kingdom and the church: 662, 1066, 1068, 1262, 1413,
1607, 2928, 3355, 4447, 4535, 5577, 8011, 9325, 9643. This is primarily because "the earth" is used to
mean the land of Canaan, and that is where the church was from the earliest times, which is also
why heaven is called "the heavenly Canaan": 567, 3686, 4447, 4454, 4516, 4517, 5136, 6516, 9325,
9327. But also because spiritually understood "the earth" means the people who are there and
their worship: 1262. Consequently, "earth" means various things that have to do with the church:
620, 636, 1066, 2571, 3368, 3379, 3404, 8732. "The people of the earth" means those who make up
the spiritual church: 2928. An "earthquake" is a change in the state of the church: 3355. "A new
heaven and a new earth" means a [new] church: 1733, 1850, 2117, 2118, 3355, 4535, 10373.

The earliest church, which existed before the Flood, and the ancient church, which existed
after the Flood, were in the land of Canaan: 567, 3686, 4447, 4454, 4516, 4517, 5136, 6516, 9325. At
that time, all the places there were given symbolic meanings related to the Lord's kingdom and
the church: 1585, 3686, 4447, 5136. That is why Abraham was commanded to go there—because
a symbolic church was to be set up among his descendants through Jacob, and a Word was to
be composed whose outermost meaning would be founded on the representative and symbolic
meanings of the names and places in that land: 3686, 4447, 5136, 6516. That is why "the earth"
and "the land of Canaan" mean the church: 3038, 3481, 3705, 4447, 4517, 5757, 10568.

---

* Swedenborg's footnotes, indicated by superscript letters, consist of references to his previously
published *Secrets of Heaven* (1749–1756). Text citations in the footnotes refer to Swedenborg's section numbers. For an explanation of these section numbers, see the list of conventions on pages
vii–x above. [Editors]

I would like to cite a few passages from the Word here that may offer some help in understanding that "earth" means the church.

> The flood gates from on high are open and the foundations of the earth are shaken. The earth is violently broken; the earth is shaken exceedingly. The earth reels to and fro like a drunkard, it totters like a hut, and its transgression is heavy upon it. (Isaiah 24:18, 19, 20)

> I will render a human more rare than pure gold. Because of this I will violently move heaven, and the earth will be moved from its place, in the day of the raging of Jehovah's anger. (Isaiah 13:12, 13)

> The earth quaked before him, and the heavens trembled; the sun and the moon were darkened, and the stars withheld their light. (Joel 2:10)

> The earth shook and trembled, and the foundations of the mountains quaked and were shaken. (Psalms 18:7, 8)

There are many other such passages.

4 Further, in the spiritual meaning of the Word "to create" means to form, to set up, and to regenerate, so creating a new heaven and a new earth means establishing a new church in heaven and on earth. You can see this from the following passages:

> A people yet to be created will praise Jah. (Psalms 102:18)

> You send out your spirit, and they are created; you renew the face of the earth. (Psalms 104:30)

> Thus says Jehovah, who is your Creator, O Jacob, and your Maker, O Israel: "I have redeemed you and called you by your name. You are mine. For my glory I have created, I have formed, and I have made all those who are called by my name." (Isaiah 43:1, 7)

There are other such passages as well. This is why our own individual "new creation" is our reformation—because we become new, and spiritual rather than earthly; and that is why a "new creation" is someone who has been reformed.[b]

---

b. "Creating" means creating anew or reforming and regenerating: 16, 88, 10373, 10634. "Creating a new heaven and a new earth" means establishing a new church: 10373. In its inner meaning, the creation of heaven and earth in the opening chapters of Genesis describes the establishment of the heavenly church, which was the earliest church: 8891, 9942, 10545.

On the spiritual meaning of the Word, see my booklet *The White Horse Described in Revelation.* **5**

The Reproduction of Humankind on Earth Will Never Cease

PEOPLE who have adopted the belief that the Last Judgment will **6** entail the destruction of everything in the heavens and on earth and that a new heaven and a new earth will come into being in their stead also believe, because it logically follows, that the reproduction and successive generations of humankind will come to an end after that. They think that all this will be over and humanity will then be in a different state than before. However, as explained in the preceding chapter [§§1–5], the day of the Last Judgment does not mean the destruction of the world; it follows, then, that humankind is in fact going to continue and its reproduction will not cease.

Many points provide support for the idea that the reproduction of **7** humankind is going to continue forever. Some of these have been presented in my book about heaven. The following points are the most relevant:

1. Humankind is the foundation on which heaven rests.
2. Humankind is the seedbed of heaven.
3. The full extent of heaven, which exists for the sake of angels, is so vast that it cannot be filled to eternity.
4. So far, heaven is made up of relatively few people.
5. Heaven's perfection increases as the number of its inhabitants increases.
6. And every divine work aims at what is infinite and eternal.

1. *Humankind is the foundation on which heaven rests.* This is because **9** humankind was created last, and what is created last serves as a base for all the [higher] things that preceded it.

Creation began from the highest or inmost things because it began from the Divine, and it proceeded to the last or outermost things and there it came to rest. (The outermost level of creation is the physical world, including our globe of lands and seas and everything on it.)

Once all this was finished, then humanity was created, and into humanity was gathered every level of the divine design from first to last. Things on the first level of that design were incorporated into what is inmost in us, and things on the outermost level were incorporated into what is outermost in us. The result is that we have been made embodiments of the divine design. This is why everything within and about us is as much from heaven as it is from this world. From heaven we get the contents of our minds and from the world we get the contents of our bodies. That is, things from heaven flow into our thoughts and feelings and cause them to take shape depending on how those things are received by our spirit, while things of this earth flow into our sensations and feelings of pleasure and cause them to take shape depending on how those things are received by our body, although only in a way that is adapted to suit the thoughts and feelings of our spirit.

[2] For material in support of this, see several relevant points in *Heaven and Hell,* particularly that the whole heaven, grasped as a single entity, reflects a single individual (§§59–67); and the same can be said for each community in the heavens (§§68–72); therefore every angel is in perfect human form (§§73–77); and this is because of the Lord's divine-human nature (§§78–86).

There is more in the chapters on the correspondence of everything in heaven with everything in the human being (§§87–102), on the correspondence of everything in heaven with everything earthly (§§103–115), and on heaven's form (§§200–212).

[3] As this design of creation shows, there is such an unbroken connection between things first and last that when we have both in view they make a single whole in which what is prior cannot be separated from what is subsequent, exactly as a cause cannot be separated from its effect. By the same token, the spiritual world cannot be separated from the earthly world or the latter from the former; so the heaven of angels cannot be separated from humankind or humankind from the heaven of angels. Therefore the Lord has provided that each does work that is of benefit to the other—the heaven of angels to humankind and humankind to the heaven of angels.

[4] That is why, even though the dwelling places of angels are in heaven and appear to be at a remove from the dwellings where we live, the angels are still right with us, in our feelings for what is good and what is true. Our seeming to be separate from them is only a matter of outward appearance, as you may conclude from the chapter in *Heaven and Hell* that deals with space in heaven (§§191–199).

[5] As for the dwellings of angels being right with us in our feelings for what is good and what is true, that is the intent of the Lord's words "Those who love me will keep my word; and my Father will love them, and we will come to them and make a home with them" (John 14:23). What is said of the Father and the Lord in this verse also includes heaven, because wherever the Lord is, heaven is there. In fact, it is the divine nature emanating from the Lord that makes heaven, as you can see in *Heaven and Hell* 7–12, 116–125.

[6] See also these words of the Lord: "The Comforter, the Spirit of Truth, dwells among you and is in you" (John 14:16–17). The Comforter is the divine truth that emanates from the Lord; this is why the Comforter is also called "the Spirit of Truth." And divine truth constitutes heaven and also constitutes the angels, because they are receptive to it. On the fact that the divine nature emanating from the Lord is divine truth and that this is what makes the heaven of angels, see *Heaven and Hell* 126–140.

This is also the meaning of the Lord's words "The kingdom of God is within you" (Luke 17:21). The kingdom of God is the divine goodness and divine truth in which the angels live.

[7] The presence of angels and spirits with us and in our feelings is something I have been granted to see thousands of times from their presence and dwelling with me. However, the angels and spirits do not know which people they are with, and the people do not know which angels and spirits they are living among. Only the Lord knows and arranges this. In a word, in heaven all feelings about things that are good and true extend outward, so people there who share similar feelings communicate with one another and are connected. In hell all feelings about things that are evil and false extend outward, so people there who share similar feelings communicate with one another and are connected. Feelings in the world of spirits extend outward very much in the way sight in our earthly world extends outward. The modes of communication are very much alike in the two places, but with the difference that in this world we see objects, while in the spiritual world we see angelic communities.

[8] We can see from this that the connection between the heaven of angels and humankind is such that each depends on the other, and that without humankind, the heaven of angels would be like a house without a foundation. This is because heaven is completed in humankind and rests on it.

The same holds true in each of us as individuals. Our thinking and our willing, which are spiritual, flow down into our sensations and actions, which are earthly, and are completed and take on a permanence there. If we did not have these latter functions as well, if we lacked these sensations and actions at our outermost boundaries, the thoughts and feelings of our spirits would dissipate like things that had no defined outlet or foundation. On this principle, when we make the transition from the earthly world to the spiritual world (which happens when we die), since we are then spirits we no longer depend on our individual base but on a communal base, which is humankind.

[9] People who do not know the mysteries of heaven may believe that angels exist apart from us and that we exist apart from angels, but I can solemnly testify on the basis of all my experience of heaven and my conversations with angels that no angel or spirit exists apart from humankind and that no human being exists apart from angels and spirits. I can testify also that the way we are joined together is mutual and reciprocal.

This leads to the prime conclusion that humankind and the heaven of angels make up a single whole and depend on each other mutually and reciprocally for their existence, which means that neither can be parted from the other.

10 2. *Humankind is the seedbed of heaven.* This assertion will be further supported in the next chapter [§§14–22], where I will be showing that heaven and hell come from humankind, which means that humankind is the seedbed of heaven.

As a preface to that, here I will state that just as heaven has been formed from humankind thus far—that is, since the beginning of creation—so it will continue being formed and enriched from now on.

[2] Now, it is within the realm of possibility that humankind on a given planet could perish. This occurs if humankind completely separates itself from the Divine, because in that case people no longer have any spiritual life, only an earthly life like that of animals. Once people are like this, they cannot be formed into a community and restrained by the bonds of law, because without an inflow from heaven, that is, without

being governed by the Divine, people become insane and, forsaking all self-control, plunge into every kind of unspeakable behavior toward each other. [3] But even if humankind were to perish on one planet by separating itself from the Divine (an outcome the Lord provides against), it would still continue on others. There are hundreds of thousands of [inhabited] planets in the universe—see my booklet, *The Earthlike Bodies Called Planets in Our Solar System and in Deep Space.*

[4] I have been told by a heavenly source that if the Lord had not come into the world, taken on a human nature on this planet, and made that nature divine, humankind on this planet would have died off and left not a single survivor today. I have also been told that the same thing would have happened if the Lord had not given us the kind of Word we have, which serves as a foundation for the angelic heaven and a way of joining it to us. On the Word as the means of joining heaven and humankind together, see *Heaven and Hell* 303–310.

However, the truth of this can be grasped only by people who think spiritually—that is, people who are joined to heaven through their acknowledgment of the divine nature in the Lord, since they are the only ones who can do this kind of thinking.

3. *The full extent of heaven, which exists for the sake of angels, is so vast that it cannot be filled to eternity.* In support of this, see the book *Heaven and Hell,* particularly the chapter on the vastness of heaven (§§415–420). **11**

4. On the fact that *so far, heaven is made up of relatively few people,* see §126 in my booklet on the planets in the universe.

5. *Heaven's perfection increases as the number of its inhabitants increases.* **12** This follows from its form, which determines the patterns in which people associate and the ways communication flows there.

Heaven's form is the most perfect form of all; and in the case of the most perfect form, the more people there are, the more there is a shared motion toward oneness among them; and they are therefore joined together more closely and harmoniously. The harmony and consequent joining together increase as the numbers increase because each new constituent there is placed between two or more others in order to connect them together, and therefore the new element provides strength and connection.

[2] Heaven's form is like the form of the human mind, whose perfection grows as the mind gains more goodness and truth, leading to greater

intelligence and wisdom. The reason the form of a human mind devoted to heavenly wisdom and intelligence is like the form of heaven is that a mind like this is in fact a miniature image of heaven's form. That is why, both for people like this and for angels, there is such complete communication of their thoughts and feelings regarding what is good and true with the communities of heaven that surround them. That communication extends farther into heaven the more their wisdom grows—that is, the more varied are the kinds of knowledge of truth that have taken root in their understanding and the greater is the abundance of desires to do good that have taken root in their will. In other words, it depends on what has taken root in their minds, because the mind consists of the understanding and the will.

[3] It is the nature of the human and angelic mind that it can be enriched more and more to eternity; and as it is enriched, it is perfected. This happens especially when people are being led by the Lord, because then they are introduced to genuinely true thoughts that become rooted in their understanding and to genuinely good desires that become rooted in their will, since the Lord is arranging everything in this kind of mind into a form of heaven—so completely that eventually it becomes a heaven in miniature.

This comparison makes it possible for us to see that the increase in the number of angels perfects heaven, because the situation in that case is much the same.

[4] Every form is made up of varied elements. A form that is not made up of varied elements is not really a form at all, because it has no characteristics and is incapable of undergoing changes of state. The characteristics of any form are determined by the way its constituent elements are related to each other, the way they interact with each other, and the way they agree to be one, which factors determine the extent to which any form is regarded as a single entity. The nature of a form is such that the more constituent elements there are that are arranged in a given way within it, the more perfect it is, because as just stated, each of its constituents strengthens, reinforces, interconnects, and thus perfects it.

[5] These facts can be better confirmed, though, by material presented in the book *Heaven and Hell,* especially where it deals with the fact that each community of heaven is a heaven in smaller form and each angel a heaven in smallest form (§§51–58); where it treats of heaven's form, which determines how people associate and communicate there (§§200–212); and where it treats of the wisdom of heaven's angels (§§265–275).

6. *Every divine work aims at what is infinite and eternal.* This is shown **13**
by many things that occur both in heaven and in this world. In both,
there is never anything that is exactly like or identical to anything else.
There is never a face exactly like or identical to any other and there never
will be to eternity. By the same token, there is no one whose character
is exactly like that of anyone else; as many people as there are—and the
same is true for angels as well—that is how many different faces and different characters there are. Despite the fact that there are countless parts
that constitute the body and countless feelings that constitute the lower
mind, no one person ever has anything exactly like or identical to what
is within anyone else. That is why every individual leads a life that differs from the life of everyone else. The same holds true throughout the
physical world and in all its details. The cause underlying such an infinite variety in absolutely everything is that everything originates in the
Divine, and the Divine is infinite. That is why there is some image of the
Infinite everywhere—so that the Divine will look upon everything as its
own handiwork, and everything, being the work of the Divine, will look
toward the Divine.

To illustrate how everything in the physical world looks toward what
is infinite and eternal, let us take just the following rather mundane example. Every seed, whether it is from a fruit tree, a grain, or a flower, has
been created in such a way that it could multiply to infinity and go on
forever. One seed leads to many more—five, ten, twenty, or even a
hundred—and each of these leads in turn to as many more. Let this fruit-
fulness from a single seed continue unchecked each year, and in just a
hundred years it could fill not only the whole surface of this earth but the
surfaces of tens of thousands of earths. By the same token these types of
vegetation have been created to go on forever. This shows us then how
they contain an image of what is infinite and eternal, and it is the same in
all other cases as well.

The heaven of angels is the reason why everything in the universe
was created, because a heaven of angels is the reason for humankind and
humankind is the reason for the heavens we see above us and the planets
they contain. So this divine work, the heaven of angels, looks above all
toward what is infinite and eternal, and therefore looks toward multiply-
ing without end, because heaven is where the Divine itself dwells. We can
conclude from this that humankind will never come to an end; because
if it did, the divine work would come to a halt at a specific quantity and
would cease to look toward infinity.

Heaven and Hell Come from Humankind

14 THE Christian world is totally ignorant of the fact that heaven and hell come from humankind. People believe that angels were created at the beginning and that this was the origin of heaven. They believe that the Devil or Satan was an angel of light who was cast out with his gang because he became a rebel, and that that was the origin of hell.

Angels are utterly astounded that this is what the Christian world believes, and even more astounded that people know absolutely nothing about heaven even though this should be central to what the church is teaching. Because this kind of ignorance has become dominant, angels rejoice at heart that it has now pleased the Lord to reveal a great deal about heaven and also about hell and by this means to dispel—as much as possible—the darkness that has been increasing every day because the church has reached its end. So they want me to assure you on their behalf that there is not one angel in all heaven who was created an angel from the beginning and that there is no devil in hell who was created an angel of light and cast down. No, all the people in heaven and all the people in hell have come from humankind. The ones in heaven are the ones who lived lives of heavenly love and faith while in the world, and the ones in hell are the ones who lived lives of hellish love and faith. Further, what is called "the Devil" and "Satan" actually refers to hell as a whole. "The Devil" means the back area of hell, where people called "evil demons" live, and "Satan" means the front area of hell, where people called "evil spirits" live.[a] On the nature of each of these hells, see toward the end of my book *Heaven and Hell* [§§536–588].

Why has the Christian world seized on this belief about the people in heaven and the people in hell? Angels have told me that it comes from a few passages in the Word understood only in their literal meaning and not illuminated and explained by means of a genuine body of teaching drawn from the Word, when in fact if the real body of teaching of the church does not light the way, the literal meaning of the Word leads the

---

a. "The Devil" and "Satan" mean the hells taken collectively, or hellish people taken collectively: 694. People who were devils in this world become devils after death: 968.

mind astray in a variety of directions, causing ignorance, heresies, and errors.[b]

Another reason people in the church have these ideas is that they believe no one will get to heaven or hell before the Last Judgment; and the picture of the Last Judgment they have adopted is that everything visible to the eye is going to be destroyed, that new things will come into being, and that souls will be reunited to their bodies, allowing people to live as human beings again. This belief goes along with another, namely, a belief in angels as beings created in the beginning, since you cannot believe that heaven and hell are from humankind when you believe that no human being will get to heaven or hell until the end of the world.

[2] To convince people that this is not the case, I have been allowed to meet with angels and have conversations with people in hell. I have been engaged in this interaction for many years now, sometimes without interruption from morning to evening; and in this way I have been taught about heaven and hell. This has happened so that people of the church will no longer remain in their misconceived beliefs about a resurrection on Judgment Day, about the state of souls in the meanwhile, and about the nature of angels and the Devil. Because these beliefs are false, they are full of darkness; and for people who base their thinking about these matters on a sense of their own intelligence, these beliefs lead to doubt and ultimately to denial. They say in their hearts, "How can such a vast heaven with so many stars, with the sun and the moon, be destroyed and disintegrate? How can stars then fall to earth from heaven, stars that are larger than the earth is? How can bodies that have been eaten by worms, devoured by rot, or scattered to the winds be reassembled and reattached to their souls, and where have these souls been in the meanwhile? What kind of experience have these souls been having without the physical senses they had in their bodies?" These and many similar

---

b. The church's body of teaching must be drawn from the Word: 3464, 5402, 5432, 10763, 10765. Without a body of teaching, the Word is not intelligible: 9025, 9409, 9424, 9430, 10324, 10431, 10582. A true body of teaching is a lamp for us when we read the Word: 10400. Any authentic body of teaching must come from people who are enlightened by the Lord: 2510, 2516, 2519, 9424, 10105. People who are focused on the literal meaning of the Word without having a body of teaching do not arrive at any understanding of divine truths: 9409, 9410, 10582. They fall into many errors: 10431. The nature of the difference between people who teach and learn on the basis of the church's body of teaching drawn from the Word and those who teach and learn solely on the basis of the Word's literal meaning: 9025.

questions, because they are incomprehensible, are not believable; for many, they even destroy belief in our eternal life, in heaven and hell, and in all the rest of the principles of the church's faith. [3] We can see this destruction taking place in people who say, "Who has come from heaven and told us that this is true? What is hell? Does it actually exist? What is this business of people being tormented by fire to eternity? What is the Judgment Day? Haven't people been waiting in vain for it for centuries?" All this and more, leading to a rejection of everything.

To prevent people who think this way—as most people do who are held to be learned and well educated because they have worldly expertise— from further distressing and misleading people of simple faith and heart and bringing about hellish darkness in regard to God, heaven, eternal life, and related matters, the Lord has opened the deeper levels of my spirit. This has made it possible for me to talk after their deaths with all the people I have ever known during their physical lives; with some of these I have talked for days, with some for months, with some for a whole year. I have also talked with so many other people that saying there were a hundred thousand of them would be an understatement. Many of these were in the heavens and many were in the hells.

I have talked with some people on the third day after they died, and have told them that arrangements were being made for their burial and funeral, which prompted them to say that they had done well in casting off what had served them for a body and its functions in the world. They wanted me to tell [their loved ones] that they were not dead but alive, and were just as human now as ever. They said they had simply crossed over from one world into another and had no awareness of having lost anything, since they had a body and sensory faculties just as they had had before; they had understanding and will just as before; they had the same kinds of thoughts and feelings, the same kinds of sensations, even the same kinds of pleasures and desires as they had had in the world.

[4] Many who have just died, on seeing that they are still people and are still alive as they were before, and in similar circumstances (since for all of us, our first state after death is much like the one we had in the world, though this changes gradually for us into either heaven or hell), are touched with a new joy at being alive and say they had not believed it would be like this. They are also absolutely amazed that they had been so ignorant and blind about what happens to us after death, and are even more amazed that people in the church have the same ignorance and

blindness, even though they of all people on the planet have access to light on such matters.c

[5] Then they begin for the first time to see the reason for this blindness and ignorance—that outward concerns, worldly and bodily preoccupations, had so completely taken over and filled their minds that they could not be raised into heaven's light and look beyond the things they had been taught, and so see what the church is really all about. When bodily and worldly things are loved as much as they are nowadays, nothing but utter darkness flows in from them when we try to think about heavenly realities beyond the teachings on faith proclaimed by our church.

A great many of the learned from the Christian world are dumbfounded when after they die they find themselves having bodies, wearing clothes, and living in houses just as they did in the world. When they are reminded of what they had thought about life after death, the soul, spirits, and heaven and hell, they feel embarrassed and ashamed. They say that their thought had been foolish and that ordinary people had been far wiser in their beliefs than they were.

Some scholars who had convinced themselves of such beliefs and had attributed everything to nature were examined, and it turned out that the outer levels of their minds were opened but the inner levels were closed. This meant that they did not look toward heaven but toward the world and therefore toward hell, since to the extent that the deeper levels of our minds are opened, we look toward heaven, while to the extent that the inner levels are closed and the outer are opened, we look toward hell. The inner levels of our minds are formed to be receptive to

16

---

c. Nowadays, few people in the Christian world believe that after we die we immediately rise again: preface to Genesis 16, §§4622, 10758. They believe instead that our resurrection will happen when the visible world is destroyed at the time of the Last Judgment: 10595. The reason for this belief: 10595, 10758. But in fact we do rise again immediately after death, and are then complete human beings in every detail: 4527, 5006, 5078, 8939, 10594, 10758. The "soul" that lives after death is the human spirit, the true self that lies within us; in the other life it has a complete human form (322, 1880, 1881, 3633, 4622, 4735, 5883, 6054, 6605, 6626, 7021, 10594); illustrated by eyewitness experience (4527, 5006, 8939); illustrated from the Word (10597). An explanation of what is meant by the dead appearing in the holy city in Matthew 27:53: 9229. How we are revived from death: 168–189 (described on the basis of personal experience). Our state after being revived: 317, 318, 319, 2119, 5078, 10596. Some wrong opinions concerning the soul and resurrection: 444, 445, 4527, 4622, 4658.

all things of heaven and the outer levels are formed to be receptive to all things of this world, but if we are receptive to the world and not at the same time to heaven, then we are receptive to hell.[d]

17   As for human spirits being people and having a similar form after separation from the body, daily experience over many years has supplied me with evidence of this, since I have seen them, heard them, and talked with them thousands of times. I have even talked with them about the fact that people in this world do not believe that they exist and that the learned dismiss as simpleminded those who do believe. The spirits are heartsick that this kind of ignorance still prevails on our globe and especially within the church. They say that this kind of belief emanates especially from the learned who think about the soul on the basis of what they sense with their physical bodies. On this basis, they cannot conceive of the soul as being anything but thought; and this, regarded apart from any subject in which and from which it exists, is to them like some volatile substance made of pure ether, which cannot help but evaporate when the body dies. However, since the church (on the basis of the Word) believes in the immortality of the soul, these thinkers have to attribute to the soul some touch of life, just as they do to thought. Still, though, they do not credit it with any human sensitive faculty until it is once again joined to its body. Their teachings about resurrection are founded on this premise; and so is their belief that soul and body will be reunited when the Last Judgment comes. What other conclusion could they come to, given their hypothesis about the soul and the need to combine it with the church's teachings concerning eternal life? That is why when people think about the soul on the basis of both that hypothesis and those teachings, they do not grasp at all that the soul is the spirit and that it is in a human form. The result is that hardly anyone nowadays knows what anything spiritual is, let alone that people who are spiritual—meaning all angels and spirits—have a form that is human.

That is why almost all the people who arrive from the world are absolutely amazed to discover that they are alive and that they are just as human as ever, no different at all. Once they get past their amazement at that, then they are astounded that the church has no idea that

---

d. The spiritual world and the earthly world are joined together in us: 6057. The inner self is formed to be an image of heaven, while the outer is formed to be an image of the world: 3628, 4523, 4524, 6013, 6057, 6314, 9706, 10156, 10472.

this is what happens to people after death, in spite of the fact that all the people who have ever lived in this world are there in the other life, leading human lives. They also wonder why people in this world have not been informed of this by means of visions. They are told by a heavenly source that this could have been done—nothing is easier when the Lord so pleases; but people who have convinced themselves of these misconceptions to the contrary would still not believe, even if they saw the visions for themselves.

These newcomers are also told that it is dangerous to disclose anything from heaven to people who have built their lives around worldly and bodily preoccupations, because they might believe at first but later reject and thereby profane the truth. Profanation is first believing something and then rejecting it. People who commit profanation are pushed down into the lowest and harshest of all the hells. This is the danger the Lord meant when he said, "He has blinded their eyes and hardened their hearts, so that they would not see with their eyes and understand with their hearts and turn, and I would heal them" (John 12:40). The Lord also indicated that people who have devoted their lives to worldly and bodily loves will not believe no matter what:

> Abraham said to the rich man in hell, "They have Moses and the prophets; let them hear them." But he said, "No, Father Abraham, but if someone comes to them from the dead they will be converted." But Abraham said to him, "If they do not hear Moses and the prophets, they will not believe even if someone rises from the dead." (Luke 16:29, 30, 31)

Another argument to support the fact that heaven comes from humankind is that angelic minds and human minds are very much alike. Both enjoy the faculties of understanding, perception, and will. Both are formed to be receptive to heaven, since the human mind is just as capable of wisdom as the angelic mind is. However, the reason the mind is not as wise in this world is that it lives in an earthly body. In such a body our spiritual mind does its thinking in an earthly way, because spiritual thinking (which we possess just as angels do) flows down into earthly concepts that correspond to spiritual ones and becomes perceptible to us in that way. It is different, though, when our mind is released from its ties to the physical body. Then we do not think in an earthly fashion anymore but think spiritually, and when we think spiritually we have thoughts that are incomprehensible and inexpressible to the earthly self—that is, we think like

18

angels. We can tell from this that our inner self, which is called our spirit, is in its essence an angel.[e]

On angels being in perfect human form, see *Heaven and Hell* 73–77. When our inner self is not open upward, however, but only downward, then although it is still in a human form after its release from the body, that form is dreadful and demonic. This is because it cannot look up toward heaven, only down toward hell.

19 The church could have known from the Word that heaven and hell come from humankind, and could have made this part of its teachings, if it had let some light in from heaven and taken note of the Lord's words to the criminal, that today he would be with him in paradise (Luke 23:43). It could have noted what the Lord said about the rich man and Lazarus, that the rich man went to hell and spoke from there to Abraham, and that Abraham was in heaven (Luke 16:19–31); and what the Lord said to the Sadducees about the resurrection, that God is not the God of the dead, but of the living (Matthew 22:32). It could also have considered the belief common to all people who are living good lives, especially the belief they have when they are nearing death and are no longer preoccupied with worldly and physical concerns: they believe that they are about to enter heaven as soon as they leave their bodily life. This is the predominant view that we all have, except at those moments when we are basing our thinking on the church's teaching regarding resurrection at the time of the Last Judgment. Ask people whether this is the case or not, and you will see.

20 Anyone well informed about the divine design can understand that we were created to become angels because the final step in the divine design is in us (see §9 above). In us something of heavenly and angelic wisdom can take form, become whole, and multiply. The divine design never stops halfway down and forms something there that has no outermost aspect. Such a thing would not be in a full or complete state. No, it goes on until it reaches what is outermost. When it comes to its outermost point, it takes on a form there, uses substances that are gathered there to

---

e. There are as many levels of life in us as there are heavens, and they are opened after death depending on the way we have lived: 3747, 9594. Heaven is within us: 3884. When we are living lives of love and caring we have angelic wisdom within; it is hidden then, though, and we become conscious of it only after death: 2494. In the Word, those people are called angels who are receptive to the goodness of love and faith from the Lord: 10528.

make itself whole, and becomes productive, which is accomplished by various forms of procreation. That is why the seedbed of heaven is on the outermost level.

This is the meaning of what is said in the first chapter of Genesis about humanity and its creation:

> God said, "Let us make humanity in our image, according to our likeness." And God created humanity in his image. In the image of God he created it, male and female he created them. And God blessed them and God said to them, "Be fruitful and multiply." (Genesis 1:26, 27, 28)

To create people in the image of God and in the likeness of God is to supply them with all the elements of the divine design from first to last and thereby make them angels at the deeper levels of their minds.

The reason the Lord rose from the dead not only spiritually but also **21** physically is that when he was in the world he glorified his entire human nature, that is, made it divine. His soul, which he had from the Father, was the Divinity in and of itself, and his body became a likeness of his soul—that is, of the Father—and therefore also divine. That is why he rose in respect to both soul and body, unlike anyone else.[f] He also proved this to his disciples. They thought they were seeing a spirit when they saw him, but he said:

> See my hands and feet—that it is I myself. Touch me and see, because a spirit does not have flesh and bones as you see I have. (Luke 24:36, 37, 38, 39)

In this way he showed them that he was human not only with respect to his spirit but with respect to his body as well.

There is more on the fact that heaven and hell come from humankind **22** in the material presented in several chapters of *Heaven and Hell,* as follows: "Non-Christians, or People outside the Church, in Heaven" (§§318–328), "Children in Heaven" (§§329–345), "Wise and Simple People in Heaven" (§§346–356), "Rich and Poor People in Heaven" (§§357–365), "Each of Us Is Inwardly a Spirit" (§§432–444), "After Death, We Are in a Complete Human Form" (§§453–460), "After Death, We Possess Every Faculty of

---

f. We rise from the dead in our spirit: 10593, 10594. Only the Lord rose from the dead with his body as well: 1729, 2083, 5078, 10825.

Sensation, Memory, Thought, and Emotion That People Have in the Material World: We Leave Nothing Behind except Our Earthly Body" (§§461–469), "Our First State after Death" (§§491–498), "Our Second State after Death" (§§499–511), "Our Third State" (§§512–520), and information about the hells (§§536–588).

All of these chapters show in specific ways that heaven is not made up of angels created in the beginning and that hell is not made up of a devil and his gang, but that both are made up exclusively of angels and devils who were born as human beings.

All Humans without Exception Who Have Been Born and Have Died since the Beginning of Creation Are either in Heaven or in Hell

23 *FIRST of all,* this follows from what was said and explained in the preceding chapter, namely, that heaven and hell come from humankind. *Second,* it follows from the fact that after life in the physical world everyone goes on living to eternity. *Third,* this means that every human who has ever been born and has died since the creation of the world is either in heaven or in hell. *Fourth,* since everyone who is going to be born from now on is also going to enter the spiritual world, clearly that world is so extraordinary in both size and nature that this physical world, where people live on various planets, cannot be compared to it.

To give a better feel for this and a clearer view of it, I would like to present and develop these points one at a time.

24 As for the fact that all people without exception who have been born and have died since the beginning of the creation of the world are either in heaven or in hell, no explanation is needed to see that *this follows from what was said and explained in the preceding chapter, namely, that heaven and hell come from humankind.*

Until the present time, the most commonly held belief has been that
we will not get to heaven or hell before the day of the Last Judgment,
when souls will be reunited with their bodies and therefore enjoy the faculties believed to belong exclusively to the body. Many ordinary people
have adopted this belief on the authority of those who have hypothesized
about the nature of what lies within us and have published their supposed
wisdom. Since these individuals give no thought at all to the existence of
a spiritual world, but only consider the earthly one, and therefore do not
think in terms of the spiritual self, they have not realized that the spiritual self each of us has within our earthly self is just as human in form
as the earthly self is. So even though they are capable of seeing that the
spiritual self is active at will throughout the earthly self and in its every
detail and that the earthly self does absolutely nothing on its own, it has
not crossed their minds that the earthly self gets its human form from the
spiritual self.

[2] It is the spiritual self that thinks and wills, since on its own the
earthly self cannot do so, and yet the thinking and willing of the spiritual
self are vital to the earthly self. The earthly self does what the spiritual self
wills, and says what the spiritual self thinks, so completely that there is no
action without some will and no speech without some thought. This is
because if you take away the thought and the will, the speech and action
instantly cease.

We can see from this that the spiritual self is the true self and that it
is present in each and every detail of the earthly self. This means that the
earthly self is an image of the spiritual self, because any part or particle of
the earthly self in which the spiritual self is not active is not alive.

Nevertheless, the spiritual self cannot be visible to the earthly self,
because what is earthly cannot see what is spiritual. What is spiritual can
see what is earthly, though: this is in keeping with the divine design, but
the reverse is not. Therefore there is an inflow from what is spiritual into
what is earthly but not the reverse; and this applies to our ability to see,
because sight flows in as well. Our spiritual self is what is called our spirit;
it is visible in the spiritual world in a complete human form, and it lives
on after death.

[3] Because the great thinkers have known nothing about the spiritual
world and nothing about the human spirit, as already noted, they have
embraced the idea that we cannot live as human beings until our souls get
back into our bodies and once again have physical senses. This has given
rise to ridiculous notions about our resurrection—that even though our

bodies have been eaten by worms and fish and have completely disintegrated into dust, they will be put back together again by divine omnipotence and reunited with our souls, and that this will not happen until the end of the world, when the physical universe will be destroyed. There are other similar notions as well, all of which defy comprehension and which the mind immediately recognizes as impossible and in violation of the divine design. So these notions have undermined many people's faith, since anyone whose thinking is based on wisdom cannot believe something that is utterly incomprehensible. There is no such thing as faith in impossibilities—that is, in things that we regard as impossible. Furthermore, people who do not believe in life after death use the absurdity of these notions as support for their denial.

Support for the fact that we do rise again immediately after death and that we are then in a complete human form is given in a number of chapters in *Heaven and Hell* [§§432–469].

I mention all this as further reinforcement for the idea that heaven and hell come from humankind; and from this it follows that all humans without exception who have been born and have died since the beginning of creation are either in heaven or in hell.

25 As for the fact that *after life in the physical world everyone goes on living to eternity,* this follows from the fact that we are then spiritual and no longer earthly, and that the spiritual self separated from the earthly retains its essential nature to eternity because our state cannot be changed after death.

Further, everyone's spiritual self is joined to the Divine, since it can think about the Divine, and can also love the Divine and be drawn to everything that comes from the Divine, such as the teachings of the church. This means it can be united to the Divine in its thinking and willing, and these two abilities *are* the spiritual self and constitute its life. Anything that can be joined to the Divine in this way cannot ever die, because the Divine is present with it and joins it to itself.

[2] For another thing, on the level of our mind we have been created in the form of heaven, and the form of heaven is from the Divine itself, as you can tell from material in *Heaven and Hell.* See "It is the Lord's Divine Nature that Makes and Forms Heaven" (§§7–12, see also §§78–86); material in §57 on the fact that each of us has been created to be a heaven in least form; "The Whole Heaven, Grasped as a Single Entity, Reflects a Single Individual" (§§59–67); and "Therefore [Every] Angel Is in Perfect Human Form" (§§73–77). In fact, our spiritual self is an angel.

[3] I have often talked with angels about this, and they have been amazed that if you look at the people in the Christian world who are called intelligent and whom others believe actually *are* intelligent, you find many who have completely discarded from their faith any idea of immortality in regard to their own life. They believe that the human soul dissipates at death just like the soul of an animal. They do not see any difference between the life in humans and the life in animals, namely, that we are able to think of things beyond ourselves such as God, heaven, love, faith, what is spiritually and morally good, what is true, and the like, and in so doing be raised up toward the Divine itself and be joined to it by all these means. Animals, on the other hand, cannot be raised above their own earthly nature to think about things like this, so their spiritual nature cannot be separated from their earthly nature after death[a] and live on its own the way our spiritual self can. This is why an animal's life is dissipated when its earthly life is over.

[4] Angels told me that the reason many of the so-called intelligent in the Christian world do not believe that their own life will be immortal is that at heart they deny the Divine and credit everything to nature instead; and people who base their thinking on this premise cannot conceive of any eternity through being joined to the Divine. As a result, they cannot conceive of any difference between our state and the state of animals, since once the Divine has been eliminated from their thinking, eternity has been eliminated as well.

[5] Angels have also said that there is within every human an innermost or highest level of life—or an innermost and highest something— where the divine nature of the Lord flows in first and most intimately. From this highest point the Lord arranges the other things within us that make up our spiritual and earthly selves, descending level by level in accord with the way we are designed. The angels called this innermost or highest something the Lord's gateway to us and his quintessential dwelling within us. They also said that this innermost or highest something is what makes us human and distinguishes us from mere animals, which do

---

a. There is an inflow from the spiritual world into the lives of animals as well, but it is a general one and not an individualized one like that of humans: 1633, 3646. The difference between us and animals is that we can be raised above ourselves toward the Lord, and can think about the Divine, love it, and thereby be joined to the Lord, which gives us eternal life; it is different for animals, which cannot be raised up to such levels: 4525, 6323, 9231.

not have it, and that this is why we, unlike animals, can have our inner levels—our higher and lower mind—raised by the Lord to himself. This allows us to believe in him, be moved with love for him, and be granted intelligence and wisdom and the ability to speak on the basis of reason.

[6] Asked whether people live forever if they deny the Divine and reject divine truths, which are the means by which our lives are united to the Divine, the angels said that such people, just like those who acknowledge the Divine, retain the ability to think and intend and therefore to believe and love the kinds of things that come from the Divine; and that this is the ability that makes it possible for them to live to eternity like everyone else. The angels added that this ability comes to people from that aforementioned innermost or highest something that everyone has. They gave extensive evidence that even the people in hell have this ability, and that it is the source of their ability to argue and speak against divine truths. That is why everyone, regardless of what they are like, lives to eternity.

[7] Since everyone lives forever after death, no angel—no spirit, even—has any thought whatever about death. They do not even know what dying is. So when "death" is mentioned in the Word, angels take it to mean either damnation, which is spiritual death, or else ongoing life and resurrection.[b]

All this has been said to make the point that all humans without exception who have been born and have died since the beginning of creation are alive—some in heaven and some in hell.

26 So that I might know that *all humans without exception who have been born and have died since the beginning of creation are either in heaven or in hell,* I have been allowed to talk with people from many ages, some of whom lived before the Flood and some of whom lived after the Flood; as well as with people of the Jewish nation known to us from the Word of the Old Testament, with some of those who lived at the time of the Lord, and with many of those who lived in later centuries right up to the present day. In addition, I have talked after their deaths with all the people I had known during their physical lives; I have also talked with little children who had died, and with many people of other religions.

---

b. When death is mentioned in the Word in connection with evil people, angels in heaven take it to mean damnation—which is spiritual death—and also hell: 5407, 6119, 9008. In the Word, "the living" mean people who have devoted themselves to goodness and truth; "the dead" mean people who have devoted themselves to evil and falsity: 81, 290, 7494. When the subject is good people who die, angels understand death to mean resurrection and ongoing life, because then we rise again, continue the life we had, and begin our eternal life: 3498, 3505, 4618, 4621, 6036, 6221.

This experience has utterly convinced me that there is not one human who has ever been born since the first creation of this planet who is not either in heaven or in hell.

Since everyone who is going to be born from now on is also going to enter the spiritual world, clearly that world is so extraordinary in both size and nature that this physical world, where people live on various planets, cannot be compared to it. This follows from the vast multitude of people who have made the transition into the spiritual world since creation first occurred and who are now all there at once, as well as from the constant increase still to come as a result of humankind entering from now on— and this without end, as was shown in an earlier chapter: "The Reproduction of Humankind on Earth Will Never Cease" (§§6–13).

[2] Several times when my eyes have been opened I have been granted glimpses of the vast multitude of people there already—so many that they could scarcely be numbered, myriad upon myriad, and this in just one section of one region. How many must there be, then, in all the rest?

You see, the people there are all gathered into communities, and there are a great many communities. Each one is in its own place and contributes to form three heavens and three hells beneath them. This means that one kind of people lives in the heights there, another in the middle elevations, another below them, and another in the lowest regions or hells underneath. Somewhat the way people in this world live in cities, people in the higher regions there live near each other, up to hundreds of thousands together. Therefore given the sheer quantity of human inhabitants there, clearly this physical world, where people live on various planets, cannot be compared to it. When someone from this earthly world crosses over into the spiritual world, it is like moving from a village to a great city.

[3] In quality as well, the spiritual world is beyond comparison with this world. This becomes clear from the fact that all the things that exist in the physical world are found in the spiritual world as well, but in addition there are countless other things there, things that have never been seen and could never be seen here. This is because all the spiritual things in that world are embodied in their own unique way in a form that appears to be earthly, and these forms are infinitely varied. The cause underlying this fact in turn is that what is spiritual is so much more exquisite than what is earthly that very little of it can be brought forth to our earthly senses, since our earthly senses cannot take in even a thousandth of what the spiritual mind takes in; yet everything that happens in the spiritual mind is presented to spirits in visible form. This is why there is no way

to describe how wonderful and stunning the spiritual world is. These characteristics are intensified, too, as the number of people in the heavens grows, since everything seen there is presented in forms corresponding to the states of each individual's love and faith and consequent intelligence and wisdom. So the variety of things there is constantly increasing in proportion to the increase in population. This is why people who have been raised into heaven say that they have seen and heard there what no eye has ever seen and no ear has ever heard.

[4] All this may serve to show that by nature the spiritual world is such that the physical world cannot be compared to it.

For more on the nature of that world, see *Heaven and Hell* where it deals with heaven's two kingdoms (§§20–28), heaven's communities (§§41–50), representations and appearances in heaven (§§170–176), and the wisdom of heaven's angels (§§265–275)—but even there, only a very few features are described.

A Last Judgment Must Take Place
Where Everyone Is Together,
So It Must Take Place in the Spiritual World,
and Not in the Physical World

28 WHAT people believe concerning the Last Judgment is that the Lord will then appear in glory in the clouds of heaven, accompanied by angels, and that he will raise from their burial places all the people who have lived since the beginning of creation. He will clothe their souls with their bodies again, and having called them all together will judge them, sending those who have done good things to eternal life or heaven and those who have done evil things to eternal death or hell.

[2] The churches have extracted this belief from their literal reading of the Word; and there has been no way to get rid of it as long as people do not realize that there is a spiritual meaning in absolutely everything the Word says, and that this meaning is the essential Word, the meaning for

which the literal meaning serves as a foundation or basis. We need to realize also that if it were not for this kind of literal meaning the Word could not be divine and serve as a source of teaching about life and faith for both heaven and the world and join the two worlds together. If we know that there are spiritual things that correspond to the earthly things mentioned in the Word, then we are in a position to know that the Lord's coming in the clouds of heaven does not mean that he will be revealed in the clouds but that he will be revealed in the Word. The Lord is the Word because he is divine truth. The clouds of heaven in which he is to come are the literal meaning of the Word, and the glory is its spiritual meaning. The angels [that will accompany him] mean that heaven is involved in this revelation; they also mean the divine truths that come from the Lord.[a] We can therefore see what these words mean—that at the end of the church the Lord is going to disclose the spiritual meaning of the Word and reveal the actual nature of divine truth. So this is a sign that the Last Judgment is at hand.

[3] On the presence of spiritual meaning within everything mentioned in the Word, even within every single word of the text, and on what that meaning is like, see *Secrets of Heaven,* where there is a detailed explanation of everything in Genesis and Exodus according to that meaning. For a collection of references assembled from that work concerning the Word and its spiritual meaning, see the booklet *The White Horse Described in Revelation.*

On the point that the Last Judgment must take place in the spiritual world and not on earth or in the physical world, this follows from the two preceding chapters, as well as from chapters yet to come. The two preceding chapters explained that heaven and hell come from humankind [§§14–22] and that all humans without exception who have been born and have died since the beginning of creation are either in heaven or in hell, so they are all together in that world [§§23–27]. In chapters yet

29

---

a. The Lord is the Word because he is divine truth in heaven: 2533, 2813, 2859, 2894, 3393, 3712. The Lord is also the Word because the Word is from him and is about him (2859); and in its deepest sense, the Word is about no one but the Lord, and focuses particularly on the glorification of his human nature, so the Lord himself is there: 1873, 9357. The Lord's Coming means his presence in the Word, and a revelation: 3900, 4060. "Clouds" in the Word mean the Word in the letter, or its literal meaning: 4060, 4391, 5922, 6343, 6752, 8106, 8781, 9430, 10551, 10574. "Glory" in the Word means divine truth as it is in heaven and as it is in the spiritual meaning: 4809, 5922, 8267, 8427, 9429, 10574. "Angels" in the Word mean divine truths that come from the Lord, because angels are receivers of those truths and do not utter them as their own but as the Lord's: 1925, 2821, 3039, 4085, 4295, 4402, 6280, 8192, 8301. The trumpets that the angels will then sound mean divine truths in heaven that will be revealed from there: 8815, 8823, 8915.

to come, we reach the point at which it is necessary to show that the Last Judgment has already taken place [§§45–52, 53–64].

30   Add to this that none of us is judged on the basis of our earthly self; therefore we are not judged while we are still living in the physical world, because during that time we are in our earthly body. Rather, we are judged on the basis of our spiritual self, so our judgment occurs when we have come into the spiritual world, because then we are in our spiritual body. It is our spiritual nature that is judged, not our earthly nature, since our earthly nature is not accountable for any blame or crime, because it has no life of its own; it is simply a tool or an instrument through which the spiritual self acts (see §24 above).

That leads us to another reason why judgment is carried out on us when we have put off our earthly body and put on our spiritual one. When we are in our spiritual body, others can actually see what our love and faith are really like, because in the spiritual world all of us are an embodiment of what we love, not only in face and body but also in speech and actions (see *Heaven and Hell* 481). That is why in that world you can tell what people are really like, and why people can be sorted instantly whenever it pleases the Lord.

From these points as well we can see that judgment takes place in the spiritual world and not on earth or in the physical world.

31   The physical life in us counts for nothing. It is the spiritual life that lies within our physical life that counts, since in its own right our earthly self is devoid of life; the life it seems to have comes from the life in our spiritual self. So it is our spiritual self that is judged. In fact, when the Word speaks of our being judged according to our actions, it means that it is the spiritual self [behind our actions that is judged]. See the chapter in *Heaven and Hell* titled "Our Nature after Death Depends on the Kind of Life We Led in the World" (§§470–484).

32   I would like to add here a secret of heaven that I touched on in *Heaven and Hell* but have not yet fully described. After death, each of us is connected to a particular community, and this is done as soon as we arrive in the spiritual world (see *Heaven and Hell* 427, 497). In our first state as spirits, though, we are unaware of this, because at that point we are still focused on what is external and not yet on what is internal. As long as we are in this state we go here and there, wherever we feel like going. In actuality, though, we are where our love is—that is, in the community of people who have the same kind of love we have.

[2] When we as spirits are in this state we appear in many different places, just as though we were physically present there. This is only the

way it seems, though, because as soon as the Lord brings us into our dominant love, we immediately vanish from the sight of others and find ourselves with kindred spirits in the community to which we have been connected. This is a unique feature of the spiritual world and bewilders people who do not understand its underlying cause.

Thus it is, then, that as soon as spirits have been gathered and sorted, they are also judged; and they all appear immediately in their own proper places. The good are in heaven, in the communities where their kindred spirits are, and the evil are in hell, in the communities where their kindred spirits are.

[3] From these points as well it follows that a last judgment can take place only in the spiritual world, both because in that world we are all an embodiment of the life that is within us, and because we are surrounded there by people who have a similar life within them—everyone is among kindred spirits. It is different in this earthly world where good and evil people can be together, neither really knowing what the other is like; here we are not spontaneously sorted out according to our life's love. In fact, none of us can bring our earthly bodies with us into heaven or into hell, so in order for us to arrive at either destination, we need to shed our earthly bodies and after that, be judged in our spiritual bodies.

That is why, as stated above [§30], it is our spiritual self that is judged, and not our earthly self.

A Last Judgment Occurs When the Church Is at Its End, and the Church Is at Its End When There Is No Faith Because There Is No Caring

THERE are many reasons why a Last Judgment occurs when the church is at its end. The main one is that when this happens the equilibrium between heaven and hell begins to fail—and with that equilibrium goes our freedom, and once our freedom is gone, we can no longer be saved. We are then quite willingly carried away to hell; and, not being in a state of freedom, we cannot be led to heaven. This is because no one can be reformed without freedom, and all our freedom comes from the equilibrium between heaven and hell. Two chapters from *Heaven and Hell* support this point: one dealing with the equilibrium between heaven and hell (§§589–596) and one dealing with our being in a state of freedom because of this balance between heaven and hell (§§597–603). It also says there that without freedom no one can be reformed [§598].

34   We can conclude that the equilibrium between heaven and hell begins to fail when the church comes to an end from the fact that heaven and hell come from humankind (see the chapter on that subject above [§§14–22]); and when there are few people entering heaven and many entering hell, the evil on the one side outstrips the good on the other, because the growth of hell entails a corresponding growth of evil. Everything evil within us comes from hell and everything good comes from heaven. Since evil is outstripping good as the church comes to an end, everyone is then judged by the Lord, the evil are separated from the good, and everything is put back into order; a new heaven is set up, and a new church on earth as well, and in this way equilibrium is restored.

This, then, is what the term *Last Judgment* refers to. It will be described in more detail in later pages [§§45–52].

35   It is common knowledge, based on the Word, that a church comes to an end when there is no longer any faith within it. It is not yet widely known, however, that there is no faith if there is no caring. I will therefore need to say more about this just below [§36].

The Lord foretold that there would be no faith at the end of the church:

> When the Son of Humanity comes, will he find faith on the earth? (Luke 18:8)

He also foretold that there would be no love:

> At the close of the age, lawlessness will abound and the love of many will grow cold; and this gospel will be preached in all the world, and then the end will come. (Matthew 24:12, 14)

"The close of the age" is the last time of the church. In this chapter in Matthew the Lord describes the steadily declining state of the church's love and faith; but the description is couched entirely in correspondences. So there is no way to understand what the Lord foretold there apart from a knowledge of the spiritual meaning that corresponds to the details of the chapter. That is why the Lord has made it possible for me to explain everything in that chapter, as well as some of the things that are said later about the close of the age, his Coming, the successive stages of the devastation of the church, and the Last Judgment, in *Secrets of Heaven* (§§3353–3356, 3486–3489, 3650–3655, 3751–3757, 3897–3901, 4056–4060, 4229–4231, 4332–4335, 4422–4424, 4635–4638, 4661–4664, 4807–4810, 4954–4959, 5063–5071).

Here I will take up the fact that there is no faith when there is no caring. People presume that faith continues to exist as long as there is belief in what the church teaches, so faith is present in people who believe. Simply believing, though, is not faith. Instead, faith is to will and to put into practice what we believe. When the teachings of the church are only believed they are not embodied in our lives. They are present only in our memory and in the thinking of our outer selves. They do not come into our lives until they come into our will and from there into our actions. Then for the first time those teachings become part of our spirit, since our spirit (whose life is the life itself that is within us) is made up of our will, and of our thinking to the extent that this thinking issues from our will. Our memory and the thinking based on it is only a waiting room where teachings first gain entrance to us.

[2] It is all the same whether you say "will" or "love," since we all love what we will and will what we love. Further, our will is the part of us that is receptive to love, and our understanding, whose function is thinking, is the part of us that is receptive to faith.

We can know, think, and understand all kinds of things, but when we are left to ourselves and weigh things on the basis of our will and love, then we discard anything that does not agree with our will or love. We therefore discard such things after our bodily life as well, when we are living in the spirit, since as just noted only what has entered into our will and love persists in our spirit. After death everything else seems alien to us, something that we throw out of the house and reject completely, because it is not consonant with our love. [3] It is quite another matter if we do not merely believe the teachings of the church that are drawn from the Word but also will them and do them. Then our faith becomes real. Faith is a passion for truth that comes from wanting to do what truth teaches because it is the truth; and wanting to do what truth teaches because it is the truth is the very definition of human spirituality. That is, it transcends our earthly nature, which involves our wanting to do what truth teaches not because it is the truth but for the sake of praise, esteem, or profit for ourselves. Truth detached from such concerns is spiritual, because in its essence truth is divine. Consequently, willing truth because it is true is the same as acknowledging and loving what is divine. In fact, this willing and

36

this acknowledging and loving are fully joined to each other and are also regarded as one in heaven. This is because the divinity that emanates from the Lord in heaven is the divine truth (see *Heaven and Hell* 128, 129, 130, 131, 132), and the people who are angels in heaven are the people who are receptive to that truth and make it part of their lives.

I mention all this to make it clear that faith is not just believing but is willing and acting; therefore there is no faith if there is no caring. Caring, or love, is willing and acting.

37 I have been shown that faith nowadays is so rare within the church that you could call it nonexistent. This was demonstrated by many individuals—scholars and commoners alike—whose spirits were examined after death to see what kind of faith they had had in the world. It turned out that all of them believed that faith was nothing more than believing and convincing themselves that something was true. The more learned among them believed that it was simply having a trust or assurance that they were saved by means of the Lord's suffering on the cross and his interceding for them. Hardly any of them realized that there is no faith if there is no caring or love. They did not even know what caring about one's neighbor is or what the difference is between thinking and willing. Most of them had gotten rid of caring, saying that caring does nothing for us, and that faith is all that is required. When they were told that caring and faith are one, just as willing and understanding are one, and that caring dwells in our will and faith in our understanding, and that separating one from the other was like separating our will from our understanding, they could not understand it. This told me that there is hardly any faith nowadays.

They were shown this very convincingly as well. The ones who were utterly certain that they had faith were brought to an angelic community where there was real faith. As soon as communication was established they clearly perceived that they themselves had no faith, and even admitted it publicly. The same thing was shown in other ways to the ones who professed faith and thought of themselves as believers but did not live according to faith, which means caring. One by one they admitted that they had no faith, because there was none of it in the life of their spirits. It was only on the outside, in some of the thinking they did while they were living in the physical world.

38 That is what the state of the church is like these days—there is no faith here because there is no caring; and where there is no caring there is nothing that is spiritually good, since the only spiritual good that can be done comes from caring. I have been told by a heavenly source that there is still some goodness among some people but that it cannot be called spiritual goodness—only earthly goodness, because for them, real divine truths remain in darkness. It is divine truths that lead us to caring, teach us what it is, and focus us on it as the goal of our striving. So caring cannot arise except to the extent that there are truths to lead us there. The divine truths, though, on which the teachings of the various churches are based focus only on faith (which is why they are called teachings of faith) and do not focus on life; and truths that focus solely on faith and not on life cannot make us spiritual. As long as they are on the outside of our lives they are only earthly—they are learned and thought about only as something remote. That is why there is nothing spiritually good these days, only the earthly good that some people do.

[2] Further, every church is spiritual at first. That is, it begins with a focus on caring; but as time goes by it strays away from caring toward faith. As a result, from being an internal church it becomes a church that is merely external. Once it becomes a merely external church, it is at its end, since it then puts the whole stress on what we know and little or no emphasis on how we live. As we individuals in that church become external rather than internal, spiritual light is dimmed for us, even to the extent that we do not see divine truth on the basis of truth itself—that is, in heaven's light, since heaven's light is divine truth. We see it only in an earthly light, and when this is by itself and not illuminated by spiritual light, we are in effect looking at divine truth in the night. Then the only grounds we have for regarding it as true is the word of some ecclesiastical authority and its acceptance by the common crowd. As a result, our understanding cannot be enlightened by the Lord, since to the extent that earthly light shines brightly in our understanding, spiritual light is dimmed; and earthly light shines brightly in our understanding when we love worldly, bodily, and earthly things more than spiritual, heavenly, and divine ones. To the extent that this is the case, we are superficial individuals.

The Christian world is unaware that where there is no caring there is no faith. It is unaware of what caring about one's neighbor is. It is not even aware that our will is what makes us who we really are, or that our thinking does so only to the extent that it draws on our willing. In order, therefore, to bring these matters into the light of understanding, I would like to append some references concerning them from *Secrets of Heaven* by way of illustration.

39

From *Secrets of Heaven*

*F*AITH. If people do not know that everything in the universe goes back to goodness and truth and that these two must be joined together if they are to accomplish anything, they also do not know that everything in the church goes back to faith and love and that these two must likewise be joined together: 7752–7762, 9186, 9224. Everything in the universe goes back to truth and goodness and to their being joined together: 2451, 3166, 4390, 4409, 5232, 7256, 10122, 10555. Truths are related to faith, and good actions are related to love: 4352, 4997, 7178, 10367.

[2] If people do not know that everything in us must—if we are to be truly human—go back to the *will* and the *understanding* and the joining together of these two, they can have no knowledge of the fact that everything in the church must go back to faith and love and the joining together of those two if there is to be any church within us: 2231, 7752, 7753, 7754, 9224, 9995, 10122. We have two basic faculties, one called understanding and the other called will: 641, 803, 3539, 3623. Our understanding is designed as a home for truths—and therefore the components of our faith—while our will is designed as a home for desires to do good—and therefore the components of our love: 9300, 9930, 10064. Thus it follows that love or caring constitutes the church; faith alone or faith separated from love and caring does not: 809, 916, 1798, 1799, 1834, 1844, 4766, 5826.

[3] Faith separated from caring is no faith at all: 654, 724, 1162, 1176, 2049, 2116, 2343, 2349, 3419, 3849, 3868, 6348, 7039, 7342, 9783. In the other life this kind of faith perishes: 2228, 5820. The teachings concerning faith alone are destructive of caring: 6353, 8094. In the Word, people who separate faith from caring are represented by Cain, Ham, Reuben, the firstborn of the Egyptians, and the Philistines: 3325, 7097, 7317, 8093. To the extent that caring wanes, the religion of faith alone gains strength: 2231. With the passage of time, the church strays away from caring toward faith, and eventually toward faith alone: 4683, 8094. In the last times of a church there is no faith because there is no caring: 1843, 3488. People who regard faith alone as ensuring salvation say that it is all right to live an evil life; yet those who devote themselves to leading evil lives actually have no faith, because there is no caring in them: 3865, 7766, 7778, 7790, 7950, 8094. Inwardly, they are consumed with false thoughts caused by their evil, although they do not realize this: 7790, 7950. This means that

goodness cannot be joined to them: 8981, 8983. In the other life they are opposed to what is good and opposed to people who are engaged in doing anything good: 7097, 7127, 7317, 7502, 7545, 8096, 8313. People who are simple-hearted know better than the wise what it is to lead a good life and therefore know what caring is, and they cannot comprehend what faith would be apart from that: 4741, 4754.

[4] The goodness [of a thing] constitutes its underlying reality, and truth constitutes its manifestation, so the truth that belongs to religious faith gets the reality underlying its life from the doing of good in a spirit of caring: 3049, 3180, 4574, 5002, 9144. So the truth that belongs to religious faith comes to life when we do good actions out of caring, which means that caring is the life within faith: 1589, 1997, 2049, 4070, 4096, 4097, 4736, 4757, 4884, 5147, 5928, 9154, 9667, 9841, 10729. Faith is not alive in us when all we do is know about faith and think about it. Rather, faith comes to life when we will to do, and actively do, what it teaches: 9224. Our faith does not join us to the Lord; what joins us to the Lord is living according to faith, which means caring: 9380, 10143, 10153, 10578, 10645, 10648. Worship in a spirit of goodness and caring is true worship; worship that is devoid of goodness or caring and is inspired only by the truth that belongs to religious faith is a superficial act: 7724.

[5] Faith alone, separated from caring, is like the light of winter, in which everything in the earth is dormant and nothing is produced; but faith together with caring is like the light of spring and summer, in which everything blooms and bears fruit: 2231, 3146, 3412, 3413. In the other life, the light of winter, which is the light of faith separated [from caring], turns into deep darkness when light flows in from heaven; and people devoted to that kind of faith then become blind and stupid: 3412, 3413. People who separate faith from caring are in darkness; they do not know what truth is and are therefore mired in falsities, and these constitute [spiritual] darkness: 9186. They plunge themselves into false convictions and therefore into evil practices: 3325, 8094. The errors and false convictions into which they plunge themselves: 4721, 4730, 4776, 4783, 4925, 7779, 8313, 8765, 9224. The Word is closed to them: 3773, 4783, 8780. They do not pay attention to or even see all the many things the Lord said about love and caring: 1017, 3416 (which include examples). They do not know what goodness is or what heavenly love is or what caring is: 2417, 3603, 4136, 9995.

[6] Caring, and not faith separated from caring, is what constitutes the church: 809, 916, 1798, 1799, 1834, 1844. How good the church would be if caring were seen as first in importance: 6269, 6272. There would be one

church—it would not be divided into many—if caring were its essential principle, and it would then not matter how people differed in the teachings of their faith and the forms of their worship: 1285, 1316, 2385, 2853, 2982, 3267, 3445, 3451, 3452. In heaven we are all evaluated on the basis of our caring; no one is evaluated on the basis of faith separated from caring: 1258, 1394, 2364, 4802.

[7] The Lord's twelve disciples represented all the various forms of faith and caring that together constitute the church, as did the twelve tribes of Israel: 2129, 3354, 3488, 3858, 6397. Peter, James, and John represented faith, caring, and good actions that come from caring, respectively: preface to Genesis 18. Peter represented faith (preface to Genesis 22, §§4738, 6000, 6073, 6344, 10087), and John represented good actions that come from caring (preface to Genesis 18). The fact that in the last times of the church there would be no faith in the Lord because there would be no caring is represented by Peter's denying the Lord three times before the rooster crowed for the third time; in a symbolic sense, Peter in that passage means faith: 6000, 6073. Both "the crowing of the rooster" and "twilight" in the Word mean the last times of the church (10134), and "three" or "three times" means what is completed (2788, 4495, 5159, 9198, 10127). Much the same is meant by the Lord's saying to Peter, when Peter saw John following the Lord, "What is that to you, Peter? Follow me, John." Because Peter had said of John, "What about him?" (John 21:21–22): 10087. Since John represented good actions that come from caring, he leaned on the Lord's chest [John 13:23–25; 21:20]: 3934, 10087. All the names of individuals and places in the Word symbolize qualities in the abstract: 768, 1888, 4310, 4442, 10329.

[8] *Caring.* Heaven is divided into two kingdoms, one of which is called the heavenly kingdom and the other the spiritual kingdom. The love that characterizes the heavenly kingdom is love for the Lord and is called "heavenly love," and the love that characterizes the spiritual kingdom is caring about one's neighbor and is called "spiritual love": 3325, 3653, 7257, 9002, 9835, 9961. On the division of heaven into these two kingdoms, see *Heaven and Hell* 20–28; and on the Lord's divine presence in the heavens taking the form of love for him and caring about one's neighbor, see §§13–19 of the same work.

[9] People cannot know what is good and what is true unless they know what love for the Lord and caring about our neighbor are, since all goodness comes from love and caring, and all truth comes from goodness: 7255, 7366. Caring is a result of knowing things that are true, being willing to do what they teach, and being moved by them for their own

sake—that is, because they are true: 3876, 3877. Caring consists of an inner desire to do what truth teaches and not in an outer desire apart from an inner desire: 2439, 2442, 3776, 4899, 4956, 8033. So caring consists of doing useful things because they are useful things to do; the quality of our caring is proportional to the usefulness of what it does: 7038, 8253. Caring is a spiritual way of life for us: 7081. The whole Word is a body of teaching focused on love and caring: 6632, 7262. No one these days knows what caring is: 2417, 3398, 4776, 6632. Nevertheless the light of our reason could tell us that love and caring are what make us human (3957, 6273) and that goodness and truth are in harmony, each belonging to the other, so the same holds true for caring and faith (7627).

[10] In the highest sense, the Lord is our neighbor because he is to be loved above all else. So everything that comes from him and has him within it is our neighbor—in other words, goodness and truth: 2425, 3419, 6706, 6819, 6823, 8124. The type of neighbor someone is is identifiable by the nature of the good that he or she does, and therefore by the Lord's presence in him or her: 6707, 6708, 6709, 6710. Every individual and every community, also our country and the church, and in the most universal sense the Lord's kingdom, are our neighbor; and loving our neighbors is doing them good out of a love of what is good, according to the nature of their state; so our "neighbor" is the well-being of others, for which we are to be concerned: 6818–6824, 8123. Our "neighbor" includes civic goodness, too, which is whatever is fair; and moral goodness, which is what is good for our life together in community. 2915, 4730, 8120, 8121, 8122. Loving our neighbors is not loving the personality they project in public but loving what motivates them from within, therefore the goodness and truth they have: 5028, 10336. If we base our love on their public personality and not on what motivates them from within, we will have as much love for evil people as for good people (3820) and we will support both the evil and the good, even though supporting evil people is harming good people, which is not loving our neighbor (3820, 6703, 8120). Judges who punish the evil in order to correct them and to protect the good from them are loving their neighbor: 3820, 8120, 8121.

[11] Loving one's neighbor is doing what is good, fair, and right in every task and in every function: 8120, 8121, 8122. So caring about our neighbor extends to every least thing that we think, intend, and do: 8124. Doing what is good and true for the sake of what is good and true is loving our neighbor: 10310, 10336. People who do this are loving the Lord, who is our neighbor in the highest sense: 9210. The life of caring is a life in accord with the Lord's

commandments; therefore to live by divine truths is to love the Lord: 10143, 10153, 10310, 10578, 10645.

[12] Genuine caring is not done to get something in return (2371, 2380, 2400, 3887, 6388–6393), because it comes from an inner desire to do what is good and therefore from a joy in doing it (2371, 2400, 3887, 6388–6393). If we separate faith from caring, then in the other life we want credit for our faith and for any outwardly good deeds that we have done: 2371.

[13] The teachings of the ancient church were teachings about how to live our lives, that is, teachings focused on caring: 2385, 2417, 3419, 3420, 4844, 6628. The ancients who were part of the church gave the good actions that embody caring a structure, divided them into categories, and gave each a name; and this was the source of their wisdom: 2417, 6629, 7259–7262. The wisdom and intelligence of people who have led caring lives in this world increase immensely in the other life: 1941, 5859. The Lord flows with divine truth into caring because he flows into our very life: 2363. We are like gardens when caring and faith are joined to each other within us and like deserts when they are not: 7626. The less we care, the less wise we are (6630); if we are not engaged in caring, we are ignorant of divine truths, no matter how wise we may think we are (2417, 2435). An angelic life consists of doing good deeds of caring, which are acts of service: 454. Spiritual angels are embodiments of caring: 553, 3804, 4735.

[14] *Will and understanding.* We have two abilities, one called understanding and the other called will: 35, 641, 3539, 10122. It is these two abilities that make us truly human: 10076, 10109, 10110, 10264, 10284. Our nature depends on the nature of these two abilities of ours: 7342, 8885, 9282, 10264, 10284. These two abilities are also what distinguishes us from animals, because our understanding can be lifted up by the Lord and see divine truths, and our will, too, can be lifted up and perceive divine goodness. And so our partnership with the Lord is made possible by these two abilities that make us who we are—which is not the case with animals: 4525, 5302, 5114, 6323, 9231. And since we surpass animals in these abilities, we cannot die with respect to our deeper levels—the levels that constitute our spirit; rather, we live to eternity: 5302.

[15] Everything in the universe goes back to goodness and truth; likewise everything in us goes back to our will and our understanding (803, 10122), because our understanding is the part of us that receives truth and our will is the part of us that receives goodness (3332, 3623, 5835, 6065, 6125, 7503, 9300, 9930). Whether you say "truth" or "faith" it amounts to the same thing, because faith and truth are mutually dependent; and whether

you say "goodness" or "love" it amounts to the same thing, because love and goodness are mutually dependent; whatever we believe we call true, and whatever we love we call good: 4353, 4997, 7178, 10122, 10367. It therefore follows that our understanding is the part of us that can have faith and our will is the part of us that can have love: 7178, 10122, 10367. And since our understanding can accept faith in God and our will can accept love for God, we are capable of being joined to God by faith and love; and anyone who can be joined to God by love and faith cannot die to all eternity: 4525, 6323, 9231.

[16] Our will is the true underlying reality of our life because it is the part of us that receives love or what is good, while our understanding is the consequent manifestation of our life because it is the part of us that receives faith or what is true: 3619, 5002, 9282. So the life of our will is our primary life, and the life of our understanding comes from it (585, 590, 3619, 7342, 8885, 9282, 10076, 10109, 10110) the way light comes from fire or a flame (6032, 6314). Whatever enters both our understanding and our will becomes part of us, but what enters only our understanding does not: 9009, 9069, 9071, 9182, 9386, 9393, 10076, 10109, 10110. Whatever is accepted by our will becomes part of our life: 3161, 9386, 9393. It follows then that we are human because of our will and our consequent understanding: 8911, 9069, 9071, 10076, 10109, 10110. We are all loved and valued by others according to how good our will is and only secondarily how good our understanding is. We are loved and valued if both our intentions and our understanding are good; we are rejected and considered worthless if our understanding is good but our intentions are not: 8911, 10076. Even after death we retain the nature of our will and our consequent understanding: 9069, 9071, 9386, 10153. Those things that are in our understanding but not in our will then vanish because they are not within us: 9282. Or to put it another way, after death we retain the nature of our love and the faith that comes from that love—the nature of our goodness and the truth that comes from that goodness—and then anything that is a matter of our faith but not of our love (or of truth in us but not of goodness) vanishes because it is not within us and therefore does not belong to us: 553, 2364, 10153. We are capable of grasping intellectually things that we would not do willingly; that is, we can understand things that run counter to our love and we have no will to do: 3539. Why it is hard for us to tell the difference between thinking and willing: 9995.

[17] How distorted our state is when our understanding and our will are not acting as one: 9075. This is the kind of state we find among hypocrites, con artists, flatterers, and imposters: 3527, 3573, 4799, 8250.

[18] Every act of will to do what is good and every consequent understanding of what is true comes from the Lord, but this is not the case for an understanding of what is true that is divorced from any act of will to do what is good: 1831, 3514, 5482, 5649, 6027, 8685, 8701, 10153. Our understanding is what is enlightened by the Lord: 6222, 6608, 10659. Our understanding is enlightened to the extent that our will accepts truth—that is, to the extent that we will ourselves to act in accord with it: 3619. Light from heaven gives enlightenment to our understanding just the way light from this world does to our eyesight: 1524, 5114, 6608, 9128. The nature of our understanding depends on the nature of the love-based truths from which it is formed: 10064. Understanding results from truths that arise from living a good life, not from falsities that arise from living an evil life: 10675. Understanding is seeing, on the basis of our experience and information, things that are true, the causes of events, their connections, and how they follow from each other: 6125. The faculty of understanding is seeing and perceiving that something is true before considering it proven; it is not the ability to prove anything we choose: 4741, 7012, 7680, 7950, 8521, 8780. Seeing and perceiving whether something is true before considering it proven is possible for us only when we love truth for its own sake—that is, when we are in spiritual light: 8521. The light that comes from corroboration is an earthly light that is available to evil people as well: 8780. Any dogma, even a false one, can be supported in such a way that it seems to be true: 2385, 2477, 5033, 6865, 7950.

Everything That Was Foretold
in the Book of Revelation
Has Been Fulfilled at the Present Time

40 NO one can know the meaning and implications of everything contained in the Book of Revelation who does not know about the inner or spiritual meaning of the Word. This is because everything that is written there is written in the same style as that of the prophetic books of the Old Testament, in which every word means something spiritual that is not visible in the literal sense. Then too, the contents of the Book of Revelation cannot be explained in their spiritual meaning except by someone who knows what actually happened to the church, including how it came to an end. This can be known only in heaven, and this is what the Book of Revelation contains. The spiritual meaning throughout the Word concerns the spiritual world—that is, the state of the church both in the heavens and on earth. That is what makes the Word spiritual and divine. That state is what is set forth in the Book of Revelation in its own order. This shows that there is no way the contents of the Book of Revelation can be explained except by someone to whom the sequential states of the church in heaven have been revealed. (There is in fact a church in the heavens just as there is on earth, and we will be talking about that some more in what follows.)

The nature of the Lord's church on earth cannot be seen by any of us as long as we are still living in this world, let alone how it has declined from being good to being evil with the passage of time. This is because as long as we are living in this world we are preoccupied with external matters and see only what is visible to our earthly self. What the church is like spiritually or inwardly is not apparent in this world; but it is clear as day in heaven, because angels enjoy both spiritual thought and spiritual sight. This means that they see only what is spiritual. Not only that, all humans who have been born since the beginning of creation are together in that world, as already explained [§§23–27]. Further, all who are there are arranged in communities depending on what kind of good they do out of love and faith (see *Heaven and Hell* 41–50). This is why angels in heaven can see both the states of the church and how they change over time.

41

[2] Now, since the state of the church's love and faith is described in the spiritual meaning of the Book of Revelation, no one can know what is implicit in all these things in sequence unless that information is revealed from heaven and unless knowledge has also been granted of the inner or spiritual meaning of the Word.

This I can solemnly swear, that the details in the Book of Revelation, right down to each word, have a spiritual meaning within them, and that in that meaning everything about the spiritual state of the church from its beginning to its end is fully described. Further, since every word there has a spiritual meaning, not a word can be left out without altering the sequence of subjects in the inner meaning. This is why it says at the end of the book,

> If anyone takes away from the words of the book of this prophecy, God will take away that person's part from the book of life, from the holy city, and from the things that are written in this book. (Revelation 22:19)

[3] It is the same with the books of the Word's Old Testament. Everything in them, every word, contains inner or spiritual meaning, so not a single word in them can be taken away. This is why under the Lord's divine providence these books have been kept intact right down to the smallest letter from the time of their composition, owing to the devotion of the many individuals who counted every detail. This was seen to by the Lord because of the holiness inherent in every subject, word, and letter, even to the smallest, in those books.

42   An inner or spiritual meaning is similarly present in every word of the Book of Revelation; that meaning contains secrets about the state of the church in the heavens and on earth; and those secrets can be revealed only to someone who is familiar with that meaning and has also been granted to be in the company of angels and to talk with them on a spiritual level. Therefore, so that what is written in the Book of Revelation will not remain hidden from human view and eventually be abandoned as incomprehensible, its inner contents have been disclosed to me. They are so extensive that they cannot be set forth in this booklet, so I intend to give an explanation of the whole Book of Revelation from beginning to end and disclose the secrets that lie within it. This explanation is to be published within two years, and will also deal with some material from Daniel that has remained hidden because of people's lack of awareness of the spiritual meaning.

43   No one who is unfamiliar with the inner or spiritual meaning can figure out what is meant in Revelation by the dragon and by Michael and his angels fighting with it [Revelation 12:3–4, 7–9]; by the tail with which the dragon drew down a third of the stars of heaven [Revelation 12:4]; by the woman who bore a male child who was caught up to God, after which the dragon persecuted the woman [Revelation 12:4–5, 13–17]; by the beast rising up out of the sea [Revelation 13:1–10] and the beast rising up out of the earth [Revelation 13:11–18], with their many horns; by the whore with whom the kings of the earth committed fornication [Revelation 17:1–18]; by the first resurrection and the second [death] [Revelation 20:4–5]; by the thousand years [Revelation 20:6]; by the lake of fire and sulfur into which the dragon, the beast, and the false prophet were cast [Revelation 20:10]; by the white horse [Revelation 19:11]; by the first heaven and the first earth that passed away [Revelation 21:1]; by the new heaven and the new earth that took the place of the first ones [Revelation 21:1]; by the sea that was no more [Revelation 21:1]; by the city New Jerusalem coming down out of heaven [Revelation 21:10–22:5]; by its measurements, wall, gates, and foundation made of precious stones, and by the various numbers involved [Revelation 21:16–21]; to say nothing of other things that are completely mystifying to people who know nothing about the spiritual meaning of the Word.

The meanings of all these things will be disclosed in the promised explanation of that book.

By way of a preliminary, I should at least mention that everything in the heavenly meaning of the Book of Revelation has now been fulfilled. In this booklet I present some general facts about the Last Judgment and the destruction of Babylon, the first heaven and the first earth that have passed away, the new heaven, the new earth, and the New Jerusalem, in order to let it be known that all these things have occurred already. The specifics cannot be presented, however, except in the context of a detailed explanation of the descriptions of these events in the Book of Revelation.

44

The Last Judgment Has Taken Place

IN its own chapter above [§§28–32], I explained that a Last Judgment takes place not in the physical world but in the spiritual world, where everyone who has lived since the beginning of creation is together; and because this is the case, no one [in the physical world] can tell when a Last Judgment has happened. Everyone expects it to happen here, believing it will change everything in the heavens we see above us, everything on this earth, and the whole of humankind. To prevent the people in the church who believe this from continuing to live in ignorance; to prevent people who think about the Last Judgment from having to wait for it forever, which will lead in time to an erosion of their trust in the things said in the literal meaning of the Word about it; and therefore to prevent many from losing their faith in the Word, I have been allowed to see with my own

45

eyes that the Last Judgment has already taken place. The evil have been cast into various hells; the good have been raised into heaven; and in this way everything has been brought back into proper order, restoring the spiritual equilibrium between good and evil, and between heaven and hell.

I have been allowed to see from beginning to end how the Last Judgment took place, as well as how Babylon was destroyed, how the people meant by the dragon were cast into the abyss, and how a new heaven was formed and a new church established in the heavens—the church meant by the New Jerusalem.

I have been allowed to see all these things with my own eyes so that I could bear witness to them.

The Last Judgment began early last year, in 1757, and was carried to completion by the end of that year.

46 It is important to know, though, that the Last Judgment was carried out only on the people who lived from the Lord's time to the present day, and not on the people who lived before that. Last Judgments have in fact previously taken place twice on this planet. One is described in the account of the Flood in the Word; the other was carried out by the Lord when he was in this world. This is the meaning of his statement "Now is the judgment of this world; now the ruler of this world is being cast out" (John 12:31), and in another passage, "These things I have spoken to you so that in me you may have peace. Take heart! I have overcome the world" (John 16:33). Then too, it says in Isaiah,

> "Who is this who is coming from Edom, approaching in the immensity of his strength, and having the power to save?" "I have trodden the winepress alone. Therefore I have trodden them in my wrath. Victory over them is spattered on my garments, because the day of vengeance is in my heart and the year of my redeemed has arrived." Therefore he became the Savior. (Isaiah 63:1–8)

There are also many other such passages.

[2] The reason a Last Judgment has taken place on our planet twice before is that every judgment takes place when the church comes to an end, as has been explained above in its own chapter [§§33–39]. On this planet there have been two previous churches, one before the Flood and a second one after the Flood. The pre-Flood church is described in the account of the new creation of heaven and earth and of paradise in the first chapters of Genesis. Its end is described in the account of the eating from the tree of knowledge, with further detail in what follows there. Its Last Judgment is described in the account of the Flood.

These stories are all written in the style of the Word that uses pure correspondences. In the inner or spiritual meaning, the creation of heaven and earth means the establishment of a new church (see the first chapter above [§§1–5]). The paradise in Eden means the heavenly wisdom of that church; the tree of knowledge means the preference for worldly knowledge that eventually destroyed that church, as does the serpent in the same story [Genesis 3:1–15]; and the Flood means the Last Judgment on the people who were part of that church.

[3] The second church, the one that came after the Flood, is also described in various places in the Word, among them Deuteronomy 32:7–14. This church spread over much of the Middle East and continued among the descendants of Jacob. It ended when the Lord came into the world. At that time a Last Judgment was carried out on all the people since the first establishment of that church as well as on some left from the previous church.

The Lord came into the world to bring everything in the heavens—and through the heavens, everything on earth—back into order, and to make his human nature divine. If this had not been done, no one could have been saved.

I have explained in various places in *Secrets of Heaven* that there were two churches on this planet before the Lord's Coming (you may see some of these references in a footnote below).ᵃ Also in that work I have explained

---

a. The first and earliest church on this planet was the one described in the first chapters of Genesis; it was a heavenly church, the finest of them all: 607, 895, 920, 1121, 1122, 1123, 1124, 2896, 4493, 8891, 9942, 10545. What the people of the earliest church are like in heaven: 1114–1125. They live in the best light there: 1117. There were several churches after the Flood, which are collectively referred to as "the ancient church": 1126, 1127, 1128, 1327, 10355. The ancient church itself was spread across all the countries of the Middle East: 1238, 2385. What the people of the ancient church were like: 609, 895. The ancient church was a church of symbolism: 519, 521, 2896. What the ancient church was like when it began to go into decline: 1128. The difference between the earliest church and the ancient church: 597, 607, 640, 641, 765, 784, 895, 4493. On the church that began with Eber and was called "the Hebrew church": 1238, 1241, 1343, 4516, 4517. The difference between the ancient church and the Hebrew church: 1343, 4874. On the church that was established among the descendants of Jacob, or the children of Israel: 4281, 4288, 4311, 4500, 4899, 4912, 6304, 7048, 9320, 10396, 10526, 10531, 10698. The statutes, judgments, and laws commanded for the children of Israel were somewhat like those of the ancient church: 4449. How the symbolic rites of the church established for the children of Israel differed from the symbolic rites of the ancient church: 4288, 10149. In the earliest church there was direct revelation from heaven; in the ancient church it came through correspondences; in the church of the children of Israel it came by audible speech; and in the Christian church it came through the Word: 10355. The Lord was God of the earliest church and of the ancient church as well, and was known as Jehovah: 1343, 6846.

that the Lord came into the world to bring back into order everything in the heavens, and through the heavens everything on earth, and to make his human nature divine.[b]

The third church on this planet is the Christian church. The Last Judgment we are now dealing with was on that church and at the same time on all the people who had been in the first heaven since the Lord's time.

47 In this booklet I cannot give the full details about how that Last Judgment was carried out—there are too many—but they will be set out in the explanation of the Book of Revelation. In fact, that judgment was carried out not only on all the people from the Christian church but also on all the people called Muslims and also on all those of the other religions on our planet; and it was done in the following sequence: first it was carried out on the people of the Catholic religion, then on the Muslims, then on the people of other religions, and finally on the Protestants.

For the judgment on the people of the Catholic religion, see the following chapter on the destruction of Babylon [§§53–64]. For the judgment on Protestants, see the chapter on the first heaven that passed away [§§65–72]. For the judgment on Muslims and the people of other religions, see this chapter [§§50–51].

48 The original locations in the spiritual world of all the religions and peoples on whom the judgment was carried out looked like this. The people called Protestants appeared gathered in the central area. They were subdivided according to their native countries: the Germans in the spiritual world were toward the north, the Swedes toward the west, the Danes

---

b. While the Lord was in the world he brought everything in the heavens and the hells back into order: 4075, 4287, 9937. At that time the Lord also freed the world of spirits from the [evil] people who lived before the Flood: 1266. What they were like: 310, 311, 560, 562, 563, 570, 581, 586, 607, 660, 805, 808, 1034, 1120, 1265–1272. Through his spiritual crises and his victories over them, the Lord gained control over the hells and brought everything back into order; and at the same time he glorified his human nature: 4287, 9937. The Lord did this on his own, or by his own power: 1692, 9937. The Lord alone did this fighting: 8273. By so doing the Lord alone became righteousness and merit: 1813, 2025, 2026, 2027, 9715, 9809, 10019. In this way the Lord united his human nature to his divine nature: 1725, 1729, 1733, 1737, 3318, 3381, 3382, 4286. His last spiritual crisis and final victory was his suffering on the cross; through this he glorified himself—that is, made his human nature divine—and gained control over the hells: 2776, 10655, 10659, 10828. The Lord could not undergo spiritual crisis with respect to his divine nature: 2795, 2813, 2814. That is why the Lord took on a human nature from his mother, a nature that can undergo spiritual crises: 1414, 1444, 1573, 5041, 5157, 7193, 9315. He drove out everything he had inherited from his mother and divested himself of the human nature he had received from her, even to the point that he was no longer her son, and put on a divine-human nature: 2159, 2574, 2649, 3036, 10830. By gaining control over the hells and by glorifying his human nature, the Lord saved humankind: 4180, 10019, 10152, 10655, 10659, 10828.

in the west, the Dutch toward the east and the south, and the British in the middle. Surrounding this whole central area where the Protestants were, there appeared the people from the Catholic religion, the majority of whom were in the western region, although some were in the south.

Beyond them were the Muslims, again subdivided by nationality. They all appeared in the southern part of the west. Beyond them people of other religions were gathered in great abundance. They constituted an outer ring; and beyond them there appeared an ocean, which formed the farthest boundary.

The arrangement of these peoples in these regions was based on each group's receptivity to divine truths. Because this is the basis, in the spiritual world everyone is known by the general region and the particular place within it where he or she lives; and in a community of many, the individuals are known by which quarter of the community they are staying in (on this subject see *Heaven and Hell* 148–149).

It is much the same when people are traveling from place to place. In every case, the route they take goes through particular regions according to the successive states of the thoughts that arise from the emotions at the core of their lives. As we will see below, that is how they are brought to the place that is their own. In short, the paths that people follow in the spiritual world are a reflection of the thoughts in their minds. This is why in the spiritual sense of the Word "paths" and "walking" and the like mean the direction and movement of our spiritual life.

In the Word the four quarters [of the spiritual world] are referred to as "the four winds," and the gathering of people from them is referred to as "a gathering from the four winds," as in Matthew where it speaks of the Last Judgment:

49

> He will send out his angels, and they will gather his chosen people from the four winds, from one end of the heavens to the other. (Matthew 24:31)

Elsewhere in Matthew we read,

> All nations will be gathered before the Son of Humanity, and he will separate one from another the way a shepherd separates sheep from goats; and he will set the sheep on his right and the goats on the left. (Matthew 25:32–33)

This means that the Lord is going to separate the people who are both seeking truth and doing good from the ones who are seeking truth but not doing good, since in the spiritual meaning of the Word "the right" and "sheep" mean goodness, and "the left" and "goats" mean truth. The judgment was not carried out on any others, since the evil who had no interest in truth were long since in hell. All the evil who at heart deny the existence of the Divine and reject all belief in the church's truths are cast into hell after they die. Therefore [such people were already in hell] before the judgment occurred.

The first heaven that passed away was made up of people who were seeking truth but were not interested in doing good; and the new heaven was formed from the ones who were devoted to seeking truth and to doing good.

50 As for the judgment on Muslims and those of other religions, which we are dealing with in this chapter, it took place as follows.

The Muslims were led from the places where they had been gathered (in the southern part of the west), by a route that took them around the Christians. They went from the west through the north all the way to the southern borders of the east, and along the way the evil were separated from the good.

The evil were thrown into swamps and lakes. Many of them were also scattered in a kind of desert on the periphery. The good, though, were led on through the east to a very spacious land toward the south and were given places to live there.

The ones who were led all the way there were those who in the world had recognized the Lord as the greatest prophet and as the Son of God and had believed that he was sent by the Father to instruct humankind, and who had also lived lives that were both moral and spiritual in accord with the principles of their religion.

[2] Many of them, once they have been taught, accept faith in the Lord and acknowledge that he is one with the Father. They are also granted communication with the Christian heaven through an inflow from the Lord; they do not mix with that heaven, however, because their religious practice differs.

The first thing all adherents of Islam do when they arrive among their own in the other life is to look for Muhammad, but he is nowhere to be seen. However, in his stead there are two others who call themselves Muhammads. They have obtained a central seat at the border of the Christian heaven, toward the left.

The reason there are these two in Muhammad's stead is that after death we all, no matter what our religion, are brought to the people we revered in the world. This is because our religion clings fast to us. Only when we realize that these people cannot do us any good do we leave them. You see, the only way we can be led away from our [false] religious beliefs is first to be brought more fully into them.

In the work that will explain the Book of Revelation I will tell where Muhammad actually is and what he is like, as well as where the two others came from.

The judgment on those of other religions was carried out in almost **51** the same way as the judgment on the Muslims, except that they were not led around in the same kind of circuitous route but rather along a sort of roadway in the west. There the evil were separated from the good. The evil were cast into a pair of vast chasms that sloped down into the depths, while the good were led over the central region where the Christians were, toward the area in the eastern quarter where the Muslims now lived. They were provided with places to live; these were behind the Muslims and beyond, stretching far out into the southern quarter.

However, people of other religions who in the world have worshiped God in human form and have lived caring lives in accord with the principles of their religion are joined to Christians in heaven, because they more than the others acknowledge and revere the Lord. The most intelligent ones come from Africa.

The number of Muslims and people of other religions I saw was so immense that it would have had to have been counted in millions. Yet the judgment on such an immense number took only a few days, because once people had been brought into their own love and faith, their true nature was instantly determined, and they were taken to kindred spirits.

These events establish the truth of the Lord's predictions about the **52** Last Judgment:

> Then they will come from the east and the west and from the north and the south and sit down in the kingdom of God. (Luke 13:29)

Babylon and Its Destruction

O N the fact that everything predicted in the Book of Revelation has **53** been fulfilled at the present time, see §§40–44 above; and on the fact that the Last Judgment has already been carried out, see the previous chapter [§§45–52]; that chapter also explains how the judgment was carried out on Muslims and people of other religions [§§50–51]. Now we turn to the way the Last Judgment was carried out on the Catholics meant by "Babylon," about whom the Book of Revelation has much to say. There is description of its destruction in chapter 18, as follows:

> The angel cried mightily with a loud voice, "Babylon is fallen, is fallen, and has become a dwelling place of demons, a refuge for every unclean spirit, and a refuge for every unclean and hated bird!" (Revelation 18:1–2)

Before describing that destruction, I wish to make some preliminary points:

1. What "Babylon" means, and what its nature is.
2. What the people of this Babylon are like in the other life.
3. Which part [of the spiritual world] they were living in until recently.
4. Why they were allowed to live there right up to the day of the Last Judgment.

[Then I will cover]

5. How they were destroyed, and how their dwellings became a wasteland.
6. How all the people among them who were engaged in doing good and had a longing for truth were saved.
7. What the circumstances are for Catholics from now on as they pass into the other world from this one.

54   1. *What "Babylon" means, and what its nature is.* "Babylon" means everyone who wants to use religion to control others. Trying to use religion to control others is trying to take control of their souls and therefore their spiritual life itself, using as means the divine principles of the religion. In a general sense, then, Babylon means all people who have control as their aim and use religion as the means of achieving it.

The reason these kinds of people are referred to as Babylon is that religious tyranny first began in ancient times, although an immediate halt was put to it. That beginning is described as a city and a tower whose top would be in heaven; its being shut down is described by the muddling of the language of those people that led to its name, "*Babel*" (Genesis 11:1–9). For what the details of this story mean in the Word's inner or spiritual meaning, see the explanation given in *Secrets of Heaven* 1283–1328.

[2] We can see in Daniel that a similar tyranny began again in Babylon, but this time became established: it says of Nebuchadnezzar that he

set up an image that everyone had to worship (Daniel 3:1–end). This is also the meaning of Belshazzar and the leaders under him drinking from the gold and silver vessels that Nebuchadnezzar had brought back from the Jerusalem temple, and worshiping gods of gold and silver and copper and iron at the same time. This is why the words "numbered, weighed, divided" were written on the wall, and why the king himself was killed that very night (Daniel 5:1–end). The vessels of gold and silver from the Jerusalem temple mean the good actions and truths taught by the church; drinking from them while at the same time worshiping gods of gold, silver, copper, and iron means profanation; and the handwriting on the wall and the death of the king mean the judgment and destruction pronounced on people who use as means to their own ends the good actions and truths taught by the Divine.

[3] The nature of people called "Babylon" is also described all through the prophets—in Isaiah, for example:

> You will take up this proverb against *the king of Babylon:* "Jehovah has broken the staff of the wicked, the scepter of the rulers. You are fallen from heaven, O Lucifer! You are cut down to the ground. You have said in your heart, 'I will ascend into the heavens, I will exalt my throne above the stars of God; I will also sit on the mount of the congregation on the farthest sides of the north; I will be like the Highest.' But you will be cast down into hell, to the lowest depths of the pit. I will cut off the name and the remnant of *Babylon,* and I will make it a possession of owls." (Isaiah 14:4–5, 12–15, 22–23)

Elsewhere in Isaiah we find,

> The lion said, "Babylon is fallen, is fallen, and all the carved images of her god have been cast down." (Isaiah 21:9)

See also Isaiah 47:1–end; 48:14–20; Jeremiah 50:1, 2, 3. From these passages we can see what "Babylon" is.

[4] It is important to know that a church becomes a Babylon when its caring and faith come to an end and self-love takes charge instead. The more free rein self-love is given, the more it rushes headlong into ruling not only over all the people on earth it possibly can, but even over heaven. Even then it does not rest; it climbs up to the throne of God and transfers God's divine power to itself.

We can tell from the passages in the Word cited above that a development like this occurred before the Lord's Coming. That Babylon, however, was destroyed by the Lord when he was in the world, both through its becoming totally idolatrous and through a Last Judgment on its people in the spiritual world. That is the meaning of the passage in the prophets about Lucifer (who is identified with Babylon there) being cast down into hell [Isaiah 14:12–15], and the passages about Babylon falling [Isaiah 13; 21:1–10; 47; Jeremiah 50–51]; the passage about the handwriting on the wall [Daniel 5:1–29] and the death of Belshazzar [Daniel 5:30–31]; and the passage about the stone hewn from the rock that destroyed the statue in Nebuchadnezzar's dream [Daniel 2:31–45].

55 The Babylon the Book of Revelation is talking about, though, is the present-day Babylon that arose after the Lord's Coming and is generally understood to be part of the Catholic world. It is actually more destructive and atrocious than the Babylon that existed before the Lord's Coming because it profanes the church's inner forms of goodness and truth, which the Lord revealed to the world when he revealed himself. What now follows will provide an overview of how destructive and profoundly atrocious it is.

[2] [The Catholic clergy] have no reverence for and acknowledgment of the Lord that possesses any belief in his power to save. They completely separate his divine nature from his human nature and transfer to themselves the divine power that belonged to his human nature.[a] They forgive sins, admit people into heaven, cast people into hell, save whomever they choose, and sell salvation. So they claim for themselves functions that actually belong to divine power alone; and since they exercise this divine power, it follows that they are making themselves gods—each one at his own level of the hierarchy, by the transfer of power from the highest of them, whom they call the vicar of Christ, to the lowest of them. By so doing they view themselves as the Lord and worship him not for his sake but for their own.

[3] They not only contaminate and falsify the Word, they also keep it from the people to deny them access to any of its light of truth. Even this is not enough—they also destroy the Word, believing in a divinity in the decrees of Rome that is superior to the divinity of the Word. So they close the way to heaven for everyone, since the path to heaven is the

---

a. The [Roman Catholic] church ascribes two distinct natures to the Lord; it separates his divinity from his humanity. This was arrived at in a council for the sake of the papacy, so that the pope could be acknowledged as the vicar of Christ. This was disclosed to me by a heavenly source: see *Secrets of Heaven* 4738.

acknowledgment of the Lord and faith in him and love for him, and the Word is what teaches us that path; and without the Lord in the Word, there is no salvation. They concentrate all their efforts on extinguishing the light of heaven that comes from divine truth so that ignorance may take its place—the denser the better, as far as they are concerned. They extinguish the light of heaven by forbidding the reading of the Word and the reading of books that contain teachings from the Word. They have made worship into masses conducted in a language that ordinary people do not understand and in which there is no divine truth; and in general they fill their world with false teachings that are darkness itself, that take away and scatter the light. They even persuade the common people that their life depends on trusting the clergy—relying on someone else's faith, that is, rather than their own.

[4] Further, they make all worship consist of an outward holiness with nothing inside it. They make the inside utterly empty because it contains no knowledge of goodness or truth. In reality, though, a ritual is only as outwardly worshipful of the Divine as it is inwardly worshipful, because outward worship comes from inward worship.

They have also introduced all kinds of idolatrous practices. They keep making more and more saints, and both see and tolerate people's adoration of them and prayers to them, almost as though the saints were gods. They display images of them everywhere; they boast of vast numbers of miracles performed by them; they devote communities and cathedrals and monasteries to them; they bring their bones out of their tombs and treat them as sacred objects even though they are absolutely worthless—in all these ways they steer the minds of all away from the worship of God to the worship of humans.

[5] Not only that, they go to great lengths to prevent anyone from emerging from that darkness into light or from the worship of idols to the worship of God. They keep founding monastic orders and stationing members of them everywhere as observers and investigators. They extort confessions of the heart, including what people are merely thinking about or wishing for, and if people do not make such confessions, they threaten their spirits with hellfire and torments in purgatory; and any who dare to speak out against the papal throne and priestly dominion are locked away in a horrendous prison that is called the prison of the Inquisition.

[6] All this is done with the sole purpose of gaining possession of the world and all its treasures and living in luxury. The clergy are the great ones, and the rest of humanity are their servants. This is not the rule of

heaven over hell, though. It is the rule of hell over heaven, because to the extent that a love of being in control gains strength in anyone—especially someone of the church—hell is in control. On the fact that this love is in control in hell and actually is hell, see *Heaven and Hell* 551–565.

This shows that what we are dealing with here is not the church, it is Babylon; because the church exists where the Lord himself is worshiped and the Word is read.

56 2. *What the people of this Babylon are like in the other life.* This cannot be clear to anyone who has not been granted by the Lord to be with people who are in the spiritual world. Since this has in fact been granted to me, I can speak of this from personal experience, for I have seen these people, I have heard them, and I have talked with them.

After death we all lead the same kind of life we led in the world. This life cannot be changed, except that the [inward] things that delighted our heart become corresponding [external circumstances] after death; there is evidence for this in two chapters in *Heaven and Hell,* §§470–484 and 485–490. So the lives of the people we are talking about here are just like the lives they had led in the world, with the sole difference that now things hidden in their hearts are revealed. These people are now in the spirit, where the things dwell that lie behind their thoughts and intentions— things they kept concealed in the world underneath a covering of outward holiness. [2] Since their inner selves are now visible, it has become clear that more than half of the clergy who have claimed the power to open and close heaven are absolute atheists. Their minds are obsessed by the power they had in the world, and that power was based on the principle that the Lord was given all power by the Father and that this power was transferred to Peter, and by the order of succession, to the leaders of the church. Consequently, there is still an oral confession of the Lord linked to their atheism. However, this lasts only as long as it enables them to have some measure of power. The rest of them, the clergy who are not atheists, are so empty-headed that they do not know anything about people's spiritual life, the means of salvation, the divine truths that lead to heaven—anything about heavenly faith and love. They believe that heaven can be granted to anyone of any sort whatever at the whim of the pope.

[3] Since we all lead the same kind of life in the spiritual world as we led in this earthly world, with no difference as long as we are not yet in heaven or hell (see *Heaven and Hell* 452–480), and since to all outward appearances the spiritual world is just like the earthly world (see *Heaven and Hell* 170–176), these people have the same kind of moral and civic

life and especially the same kind of worship, since this takes root and is firmly lodged in the deepest levels of our nature. None of us can be led out of it after death, either, except those who have been motivated by truth to do good and those who have been motivated by goodness to seek truth. The people we are talking about here, though, are harder to rescue from their form of worship than others are because these people have not been motivated by truth to do good and have certainly not been motivated by goodness to seek truth. Except in the case of a few points, their "truths" are not drawn from the Word, and the few that they do have from the Word have been distorted by being used to gain power. This means that any good they do is not genuinely good, since it is the quality of the truths we have that determines the quality of the good we do.

The reason for saying all this is to let it be known that the kind of worship these people practice is just the same in the spiritual world as it was in the earthly world.

[4] With this as a preface, I would like to relate something about their life in the spiritual world and also about the form of worship they practice there. They have a kind of supreme council that serves the function of the supreme council or consistory in Rome, where the leaders meet to confer about one or another of their religious concerns—especially how the common people can be kept in blind obedience and how their own power can be extended. This council meets in the eastern part of the southern region. However, no one who has actually been a pope or cardinal dares attend. The minds of [many] popes and cardinals are possessed with the idea that they have divine authority, because they claimed the Lord's power on earth for themselves. The moment they arrive, therefore, they are taken away and cast out to join kindred spirits in the wilderness. Any popes or cardinals who had an upright mind, however, and did not accept the church's belief that they had divine power, sit in a darkened room adjacent to where the council meets.

[5] There is another gathering in the northern part of the west. Its task is to allow lay believers to experience their idea of heaven. The leaders there set up a number of groups around themselves that enjoy various superficial pleasures. In some of these groups, people play games; in some they dance; in some they are entertained in various ways to put a smile on their face; and in some they carry on friendly conversations: over here there is a conversation about civil affairs; over there, about religious matters; and over there, about lewd subjects—and so on. Depending on the believers' wishes, the leaders send them to one or another of

these communities, referring to them as "heaven"; but in every case, after being there a few hours the believers become completely bored and wander off, because these pleasures are only shallow and superficial. In this way, many individuals are led to rethink the beliefs they had been taught about what it is to be in heaven.

[6] As specifically concerns Catholic worship there, this is very much like their worship in the world. It consists of celebrating the mass as they did on earth; they conduct it in a language that is not a common language among spirits but is composed of words that sound profound. These engender an external sense of reverence and even cause people to tremble, although they do not understand a single word they are hearing.

People revere their saints in the same way as they had and display their images. The saints themselves, however, are nowhere to be seen, because the ones whose goal in life was to be worshiped as a demigod are in hell, and the others, who had no goal of being worshiped, are in the company of ordinary spirits. The leaders know this because they themselves have searched them out and have found them—and therefore now hold them in contempt. They keep this secret from the common people, however, so that the saints may still be worshiped as godly protectors, while the leaders themselves, as rulers of the people, will be revered as lords of heaven.

[7] They establish a great many monastic orders and cathedrals there, too, just as they did in the world; and they amass wealth and accumulate valuables that they hide away in their vaults. (There are valuables in the spiritual world just as there are in the earthly world—in fact, in that world there are many more of them.)

They send out monks there just as they do here, to lure non-Christians into their religion and subject them to their control. It is a common practice of theirs to have watchtowers erected in the middle of their congregations, from which they can keep all the surrounding neighborhoods under observation. They also create for themselves various methods and means of communication with others both near at hand and far away, making treaties with them and getting them on their side.

[8] That is their state in general. As for the bishops of that religion in particular, many of them deny that the Lord has any power and claim that power for themselves; and since they do this, they do not acknowledge the Divine at all. Even so, they assume a kind of outward holiness, but a holiness that is actually profane within because of their lack of any inner acknowledgment of the Divine. As a result, they are in touch

with some communities of the lowest heaven by means of their outward holiness but with the hells by means of their inward profanation, so they face both ways. Therefore they are able to persuade simple but good-hearted spirits to join them and they set them up with places to live near themselves, and yet they also gather malicious spirits and surround the congregation with them. They join themselves to heaven through the simple but good-hearted spirits and to hell through the malicious spirits. This is how they are able to carry out unspeakable things perpetrated from hell. These simple but good-hearted spirits, though, who live at the boundaries of heaven, do not look beyond the outward holiness [of these bishops], and notice only the extreme holiness of their outward worship of the Lord. They are unaware of the bishops' crimes and therefore think well of them. This good opinion provides the bishops with their best form of protection. Eventually, though, with the passage of time, all these bishops lapse from their outward holiness, and are then separated from heaven and cast into hell.

[9] This may give you some idea of what the people of this Babylon are like in the other life.

I realize that some people are going to wonder whether things like this really happen in the spiritual world—people who have a worldly focus and whose only ideas of our state after death and of heaven and hell are meaningless and empty. But things stated and explained in *Heaven and Hell* on the basis of what I have heard and seen establish that we are still human after death, that we are in the company of other people there as we were in this world, and that we live in houses [§§183–190], hear sermons in church [§§221–227], do our work [§§387–394], and see the same kinds of things in that world as we did in the world we left behind [§§170–176].

I talked with some Catholics about the keys that were given to Peter, and asked whether they believed that the Lord's power over heaven and hell was actually transferred to Peter. Since this was a fundamental principle of their religious system, they vehemently insisted on it, saying that there was no doubt whatever about it because Scripture clearly said so. However, when they were asked whether they were aware that there is a spiritual meaning within the details of the Word, which is the meaning that the Word has in heaven, at first they said that they were not aware of this. Later, though, they said that they would look into it; and when they did, they were taught that within the details of the Word there is a spiritual meaning that differs from the literal meaning the way anything spiritual differs from what is

57

earthly. They were also taught that no individual who is mentioned by name in the Word is mentioned by name in heaven, but that instead of the name something spiritual is indicated. Then they were told that "Peter" in the Word means the truth of the church's faith that teaches good actions done out of caring. "The rock" that is mentioned there in connection with Peter has the same meaning, since it says, "You are Peter, and on this rock I will build my church" (Matthew 16:18 and following). This does not mean that power was given to Peter but that power belongs to the truth that serves the doing of good, since all power in the heavens belongs to truth acting on behalf of what is good, or to goodness acting through the agency of truth. Further, since everything good and everything true comes from the Lord and none of it from us, we can see that all power belongs to the Lord.

They became angry when they heard this and said they wanted to know whether there really was a spiritual meaning in these particular words, so the Word as it exists in heaven was given to them. In that form of the Word there is a spiritual meaning but no meaning that is earthly, because it is for angels, who are spiritual beings (on this as the nature of the Word in heaven, see *Heaven and Hell* 259, 261). When they read this passage in it, they saw very clearly that instead of Peter it mentioned truth from the Lord that teaches the doing of good.[b] When they saw this they angrily rejected that Word. If it had not been taken away at that moment they might very well have shredded it with their teeth. In this way they were convinced— even though they did not want to be convinced—that only the Lord has that power. No human has it at all, because it is a divine power.

---

b. The Lord's twelve disciples represented all the various forms of truth and goodness, or of faith and love, that together constitute the church, as did the twelve tribes of Israel: 2129, 3354, 3488, 3858, 6397. Peter, James, and John represented faith, caring, and good actions that come from caring, respectively: preface to Genesis 18. Peter represented faith: preface to Genesis 22, §§4738, 6000, 6073, 6344, 10087. Peter's being given the keys of the kingdom of heaven means that all power belongs to the truth that teaches the doing of good, or to the faith that teaches the caring that comes from the Lord; so all power belongs to the Lord: 6344. The "key" means the power of opening and closing heaven: 9410. All power belongs to goodness acting through the agency of truth, or to truths acting on behalf of what is good, which come from the Lord: 3091, 3563, 6344, 6423, 6948, 8200, 8304, 9327, 9410, 9639, 9643, 10019, 10182. "Peter" in the Word means the Lord's divine truth: 8581, 10580. All the names of individuals and places in the Word symbolize qualities and states: 768, 1888, 4310, 4442, 10329. These names do not enter heaven but change into the things that they mean; in fact, these names cannot even be pronounced in heaven: 1876, 5225, 6516, 10216, 10282. The elegance of the Word's spiritual meaning where the literal text consists of nothing but names: 1224, 1264, 1888 (which include examples).

3. *Which part of the spiritual world they were living in until recently.* I **58** mentioned in §48 above what the original locations in the spiritual world of all the religions and peoples looked like, as follows: the people called Protestants appeared gathered in the central area; surrounding this central area were the people from the Catholic religion; beyond them were the Muslims; and finally there were the people of the various other religions. This shows that the Catholics constituted a ring immediately surrounding the Protestants, who were in the central area. The reason for this proximity is that the people in the central area are in the light of truth from the Word, and people who are in the light of truth from the Word are in heaven's light. This is because heaven's light comes from divine truth, and the Word is what contains that truth. On heaven's light coming from divine truth, see *Heaven and Hell* 126–140; and on the Word being divine truth, see *Heaven and Hell* 303–310. The light that is in the center radiates outward toward the circumference and illuminates it. The people from the Catholic religion immediately surround the central area, then, because they too have the Word and because it is read by members of their ecclesiastical hierarchy, although not by their laity. So this is why Catholic people in the spiritual world have homes near those who are in the light of truth from the Word.

[2] Now I need to need to say what their life was like before their homes were completely destroyed and laid waste.

Most of the Catholics lived in the southern and the western regions— relatively few were in the northern and the eastern regions.

The ones who lived in *the south* were [clergy] who in the world had been more clever than others and who had firmly convinced themselves of their religious principles. Among them also lived many of the nobility and the wealthy; these did not live above ground there but lived underground for fear of robbers, stationing guards at the entrances. There was a vast city in that region, one that stretched almost all the way from east to west and even extended a little into the west itself, situated close to the central area where the Protestants lived. Millions of people (or spirits) were living in that city. It was full of cathedrals and monasteries. The clergy would bring into the city all the treasures they had been able to accumulate and would hide them away in their own basements or else in underground vaults. These vaults were constructed in such a way that no one but they could get in—they were laid out in the form of a maze. The clergy set their hearts on this treasure hoard, and were convinced it would never be destroyed to all eternity. I have seen the vaults; I was amazed at the skill with which they had been constructed and endlessly extended. Many of those who call themselves members of the Society of Jesus were there; they cultivated friendly relationships with the wealthy who lived in the surrounding areas.

On the eastern side of that region there was a place of council, where clergy would meet to discuss how to extend their own power and how to keep the common people in blind obedience, as noted in §56 above. All of this concerns the Catholic dwelling places in the southern region.

[3] The Catholics who lived in *the north* were the ones who were not as clever and were less firmly convinced of their religious principles because the sight of their minds was dull, which meant that they were people of blind faith. The population there was not as great as in the south. Most of them lived in a major city that reached from the border with the east toward the west, and even a little way into the west itself. This city too was full of cathedrals and monasteries. On its eastern edge there were many people of various different religions, including some Protestants. A few places in that region but outside the city were also occupied by Catholics.

[4] The Catholics who lived in *the east* were the individuals of that denomination who had taken the greatest delight in being in power in the world and also possessed some earthly enlightenment. In the spiritual world, they appeared on mountains, but only on the side of them that faced north. None at all were on the side that faced south. On the border of the northern region there was a mountain, and on top of it they stationed a person who was spiritually deranged. By means of a form of thought-communication well known in the spiritual world but unknown on earth, Catholic leaders were able to inspire him to issue any commands they wished, proclaiming that he was the actual God of heaven in human form, and directing all divine worship toward him. They invented this device to keep the laity obedient, since the latter kept trying to distance themselves from the idolatrous worship the leaders promoted. [5] This is the mountain meant by "the mountain of the congregation on the farthest sides of the north" in Isaiah 14:13; the people on that mountain are the ones meant by "Lucifer" (Isaiah 14:12), since the ones from the Babylonian crew on the east were the ones who had the most light— a light they in fact skillfully procured for themselves. I have even seen some who were building a tower to reach all the way to heaven, where the angels live; but this was just a representation of their schemes. In the spiritual world schemes are presented to the eyes of people who are at a

distance as things that are not actually happening for the ones who are doing the scheming. This is quite common there. This particular sight made it possible for me to know the meaning of the *tower whose head was in heaven, so the place was called "Babel"* (Genesis 11:1–10). This is what Catholics were doing in the eastern region.

[6] *The west,* toward the front, was inhabited by people from that religion who had lived during the Dark Ages—many of them lived underground there, one generation beneath another. A whole tract toward the front, facing north, had apparently been hollowed out underneath and was full of monasteries. You could see their entrances, through caves with covers over them. The people went out and in through these caves, but rarely talked with those who had lived in later ages. These earlier people were of a different disposition and not so evil minded, because in their times there were no Protestants to fight with, so they had not engaged in so much trickery and malice prompted by hatred and vengefulness.

In a western region beyond this tract there were many mountains where the most vicious of these people lived, ones who at heart denied the Divine and yet surpassed all others in their verbal professions of reverence and their devout behavior. The people who lived there devised unspeakably horrible methods of keeping the laity under the yoke of their tyranny, and of coercing others as well to submit to that yoke. I am not free to describe these methods, because they were horrendous; but they were like the schemes described in very general terms in §580 of *Heaven and Hell.* [7] The mountains they lived on are meant by the seven mountains mentioned in the Book of Revelation, and the people themselves are described there as the woman sitting on a scarlet beast, as follows:

> I saw a woman sitting on a scarlet beast that was full of names of blasphemy, having seven heads and ten horns. She had a name written on her forehead: "Mystery, Babylon the Great, the Mother of Fornications and of the Abominations of the Earth." The seven heads are seven mountains on which the woman sits. (Revelation 17:3, 5, 9)

In the inner meaning, a woman means the church; in an opposite sense, as here, a woman means a profane kind of religion. The scarlet beast means the profanation of heavenly love, and the seven mountains mean a profane love of power. So this is how Catholics were living in the western region.

[8] The reason Catholics live in several different regions is that in the spiritual world we are all taken to the region, and the place within that

region, that corresponds to our own feelings and loves. No one is taken anywhere else. For more on this point, see the chapter that deals with the four quarters in heaven, in *Heaven and Hell* 141–153.

[9] In general, all the deliberations of the people of this Babylon focus on ruling not only over heaven but over the entire earth as well, with the aim of taking possession of both heaven and earth, using their stake in each to help them conquer the other. To accomplish this they are constantly thinking up and coming out with new rules and new edicts. They work at this in the other life much the way they did in the world, since we are all the same kinds of people after death as we were in the world, especially in regard to our religion. It was granted me to hear some of their leaders coming up with edicts that were designed to be normative for the common people. There were many separate articles, but they all had the same aim: to increase the leaders' power over the heavens and over the earth, to the point where they would have all the power, and the Lord would have none. These edicts were later read before lay people who were present, and when the reading ended, they heard a voice from heaven saying that though the leaders had not realized it, the content had been dictated by the lowest hell. This was confirmed, too, by the fact that a crew of demons came up from that hell, pitch black and dreadful, snatched these edicts away not with their hands but with their teeth, and carried them back down into their hell. The lay people who saw this were shocked.

59 4. *Why they were allowed to live there right up to the day of the Last Judgment.* This is because the divine design calls for keeping out [of hell] all the people who can possibly be kept out, and doing so until they can no longer remain among the good. So all are kept out who are capable of pretending outwardly to lead a spiritual life—to represent it in moral behavior as though spirituality were really there inside them, no matter what the faith and the love inside them are actually like. Likewise, people who maintain an outward holiness are kept out [of hell] even if they have no inner holiness. Many of the Catholic leaders were of this kind. That is, they were able to say pious things to lay people, show holy reverence to the Lord, sow the seeds of religion in their minds, induce them to think about heaven and hell, and by preaching the importance of how we live inspire them to concentrate on doing what is good. These leaders were able to lead many people to a life of doing good and thereby set them on the path to heaven. This means that many lay adherents of that religion were saved, even though few of the leaders were. These leaders were of the type the Lord referred to as "false prophets, who come in sheep's clothing but inwardly are ravenous wolves" (Matthew 7:15). [2] In the inner meaning of the Word, "prophets" mean people who teach what is true and use truths to lead others to the doing of good, and "false prophets" mean those who teach what is false and use bad teachings to lead people astray. They are just like the scribes and Pharisees whom the Lord described in the following words:

> They sit in Moses' seat. Observe and do everything they tell you to observe, but do not act in accordance with their deeds, because they say but do not do. Everything they do is to be seen by others. They close the kingdom of the heavens to others, and they themselves do not go in either. They devour widows' houses and for appearance's sake pour out long prayers. Woe to you, hypocrites! You cleanse the outside of the cup and the plate, but inside they are full of extortion and unrighteousness. Cleanse the inside of the cup and the plate first, so that the outside of them may be clean as well. You are like whitewashed tombs that look beautiful outwardly, but are inwardly full of dead people's bones. Even so you also look righteous to others outwardly, but are inwardly full of hypocrisy and unrighteousness. (Matthew 23:1–28)

[3] Another reason they were allowed to stay is that after death we all maintain the religion in which we were steeped in the world; so we become immersed in it again as soon as we arrive in the other life. Among Catholics the religion was instilled by leaders who made a display of holiness in their words and imitated it in their behavior, and impressed on lay people the belief that the leaders had power over their salvation. This, then, is another reason why leaders like this were not taken away from the laity but were kept among them.

[4] The main reason, though, is that in the time between one judgment and the next, all the individuals are kept together who have led seemingly spiritual lives in outward matters and who have modeled reverence and holiness as though it were within them. Common people can be taught and led by leaders like this. After all, people of simple faith and heart do not look any deeper than the outside that they can see with their own eyes. That is why all such people from the beginning of the Christian church right up to Judgment Day have been allowed to stay. I have already explained [§46] that Last Judgments have happened twice before and that this one is the third. All these people are the ones who made up the "first heaven," the ones meant in Revelation 20:5–6 by those who had no part in the first resurrection. Because they were as described above

[§§54–56], that heaven was destroyed, and those who were hoping for a second resurrection were cast out.

[5] It is important to note, however, that the only [evil] people who were kept out of hell were those who had allowed themselves to be restrained by both civil and spiritual laws, because they were the ones who were capable of living with others in society. [Evil] people who could not be kept in restraint by these laws were cast into hell long before the day of the Last Judgment, because communities are constantly being cleansed and purged of people like this. So if church leaders have led criminal lives, enticed lay people to do evil things, and practiced unspeakable arts of the kind used by those in hell (see *Heaven and Hell* 580), they are cast out of their communities; but they go back and forth. [6] Likewise, individuals who are inwardly good are also taken away from these communities so that they will not be contaminated by the ones who are inwardly evil. The good perceive what lies within others and therefore do not focus on their superficial traits except to the extent that these reflect inner ones. Before the judgment they are taken back and forth to places of instruction (see *Heaven and Hell* 512–520); from there they are finally brought into heaven. These are the people who make up the new heaven and are meant by those who have a part in the first resurrection.

I mention this to let it be known why so many leaders from the Catholic religion were tolerated and kept around right up to the day of the Last Judgment. But more on the same subject will be said in the next chapter [§§65–72], which will deal with the first heaven that passed away.

60 5. *How they were destroyed, and how their dwellings became a wasteland.* This I would like to describe briefly here—there will be more in my explanation of the Book of Revelation.

No one else could know that the Babylon we are dealing with here was destroyed except someone who actually saw it happen. I have been allowed to see how the Last Judgment on all the peoples happened and how it was carried out, and particularly how it was carried out on the people of this Babylon. Therefore I will provide a description. The main reason this was granted to me was to reveal to the world that all the predictions in the Book of Revelation are divinely inspired and that it is a prophetic book of the Word. If this were not revealed to the world along with the inner meaning (which is contained in its details just as inner meaning is contained in the details of the prophetic books of the Old Testament), the Book of Revelation could be rejected as incomprehensible. A corollary would be disbelief—a conviction that what is said in it is not worthy of belief and therefore there is not going to be any Last Judgment. (The people [on earth] who are part of this Babylon are more susceptible to this point of view than anyone else.) Therefore to prevent all this from happening, it has pleased the Lord to make me an eyewitness.

However, I cannot present here everything I have seen about the Last Judgment on the people of Babylon or the destruction of that Babylon itself. I have seen so much that it would fill a large volume, so all I will be doing here is offering some general impressions, leaving the details for the explanation of the Book of Revelation.

Since the people of this Babylon had settled in and were spread out across a number of different areas in the spiritual realm and had formed communities in all four regions there (as explained in §58 above), I would like to describe how that destruction took place in each region.

The destruction came about after a process of spiritual assessment, **61** because there is always an initial assessment of this kind. The assessment process involves both an investigation of what people are really like and also a separation of the good from the evil; the good are taken away and the evil are left behind.

Once this process was complete, immense earthquakes occurred, which made people aware that the Last Judgment was at hand. Everyone was then seized with trembling.

Next I saw the people who lived in *the southern region,* especially the ones who lived in the major city mentioned in §58 above, running in all directions. Some were running to escape, some were running to hide in the vaults, some were running to hide in the basements or pits where they kept their wealth, some were running away from those places carrying everything they had been able to lay their hands on. After the earthquakes, though, there was an eruption from beneath that overturned everything in the city and in the area around it. After the eruption came a powerful wind from the east, which stripped everything, shook everything, and turned everything upside down. Then everyone there was brought out from every locale and every hiding place and cast into an ocean whose waters were black. Millions of people there were thrown in.

[2] Next a smoke rose up from that whole region, the kind that rises after a major fire. Then a cloud of heavy dust rose into the air and was blown by the east wind out onto the ocean, covering its surface. Their wealth had been turned into this dust, all the possessions they called sacred because they were theirs. The dust was deposited on the ocean because this kind of dust means something that has been condemned.

[3] At the end, I saw some black creature flying over that whole region. On closer view it looked like a dragon, a sign that that whole great city and that whole region had been turned into a wilderness. The reason for this image was that dragons mean the false teachings of that kind of religion, and their den means the wilderness that follows an overthrow. See Jeremiah 9:11; 10:22; 49:33; Malachi 1:3.

[4] I also saw that some [of the clergy] had what looked like a millstone around their left arms. This was a symbol of the fact that they had used the Word to support their own loathsome dogmas. That is the sort of thing meant by a millstone. I could see from this what it means in Revelation when it says,

> An angel took up a stone like a great millstone and threw it into the sea, saying, "Thus with violence the great city Babylon will be thrown down and will not be found anymore." (Revelation 18:21)

[5] It was different, though, for the people who were in the place of council, in the same region but more toward the east, the council where clergy would meet to discuss how to extend their own power and how to keep the common people in ignorance and blind obedience (on this council see §58 above). These people were cast not into the black ocean but into a great chasm that opened up far and deep beneath them and around them.

That is how the Last Judgment was carried out on the people of this Babylon in the southern region.

[6] The following, though, is how the Last Judgment was carried out on the people who lived *toward the front of the western region* and the ones who lived in *the northern region,* where there was that other major city.

After massive earthquakes that uprooted everything there right down to the foundations (these, not earthquakes on earth, are the earthquakes referred to in the Word: see Matthew 24:7; Luke 21:11, and similar mentions in Revelation 6:12; 8:5; 11:13; 16:18, and in the Old Testament prophets), an east wind came from the south through the west into the north and laid that whole region bare—first the region toward the front of the western quarter, where the people who had lived during the Dark Ages were dwelling underground, and then the great city that stretched from that quarter all the way through the north to the east. Once all the surfaces had been stripped away, everything that had been hidden there became visible. However, since there was not as much wealth there, I saw no eruption or sulfurous fire consuming treasures. There was only upheaval and destruction, and then everything would turn to smoke. The east wind would die down and then come back again, overturning and destroying things, and carrying them away. [7] It carried off hundreds of thousands of monks and commoners, and cast some of them into the part of the black ocean that borders the west. Some others were cast into the great southern abyss mentioned just above, and some into a great chasm in the west. Still others were cast into a non-Christian hell, since a number of the people who had lived in the Dark Ages were as idolatrous as non-Christians. I could also see smoke rising up from that area, going all the way out to the ocean, floating down onto it, and creating a black crust on top of it. The part of the ocean the people had been cast in became completely covered in the dust and ashes of their former homes and possessions. As a result that ocean was no longer visible; instead there was black earth there, under which were their hells.

[8] The Last Judgment on the people who lived on mountains in *the eastern region* (see §58 above on them as well) was carried out like this. I saw those mountains sink into the depths, and all the people on them were swallowed up. The person they had stationed on top of the one mountain there and had proclaimed as God grew darker and darker and then burst into flames and was cast headlong into hell along with the rest. The monks of various orders who lived on those mountains had been calling him God and themselves Christ; in fact, wherever they went they maintained the appalling conviction that they were Christ.

[9] Finally, a judgment was carried out on the people who lived farther out in *the western region,* on mountains there. They were the people meant by the woman sitting on a scarlet beast whose seven heads were seven mountains (also described in §58 above). I saw some of their mountains split down the middle, revealing a huge chasm that spiraled downward; those who were on those mountains were hurled into that chasm. Other mountains were torn up by the roots and turned completely upside down, so that what had been the peak became the bottom of the mountain. The people from that region who were out on the plains were inundated by a flood and submerged; and the people who were there from other regions were cast into chasms.

What I have just been saying, though, is only a fraction of everything I saw. I will be offering more in the explanation of the Book of Revelation.

These things happened and were completed early in 1757.

[10] As for the *chasms* into which everyone was cast except for the people who were thrown into the black ocean, there are many, of which

I was shown four. There was a huge one in the southern region, toward the east there; another in the western region, toward the south there; a third also in the western region, but toward the north there; and a fourth farther out, on the border between the west and the north. The chasms and the ocean are their hells.

I saw these chasms, but there were many more that I did not see. The hells of the people of Babylon are divided up according to the various ways in which they profane spiritual things that have to do with the truth and the goodness that are taught by the church.

62 So the world of spirits has now been freed from people like this, and the angels are overjoyed at this liberation, because the people of Babylon were burdening and leading astray as many as they could, even more there than they had in the world. This was because their trickery was more vicious in that world, since they were now spirits, and any malice in someone hides itself within that person's spirit, because the spirit in each of us is the part that thinks, intends, strives, and plans. Many of them were examined and were found to believe nothing at all. Their minds were found to be obsessed with a heinous desire to lead people astray—doing so to the rich in order to gain their wealth and to the poor in order to gain power. Because this was their purpose they kept everyone in the deepest ignorance and closed off the way to the light and therefore to heaven. The way to the light and to heaven is closed off when knowledge of spiritual things is buried under idolatrous practices and the Word is contaminated, weakened, or taken away altogether.

63 6. *How all the people among them who were engaged in doing good and had a longing for truth were saved.* Catholics who had lived reverent lives and were devoted to doing good and who, although they did not know truths, felt a longing to know them, were rescued and brought to a particular area toward the front of the western region on its border with the north. There they were given places to live and were established in communities. Then they were sent some Protestant clergy to teach them the Word, and as they learned it they were received into heaven.

64 7. *What the circumstances are for Catholics from now on as they pass into the other world from this one.* Since the Last Judgment has now been carried out and the Lord has brought everything back into order, and since all the people who were inwardly good have been taken up into heaven and all the ones who were inwardly evil have been cast down into hell, it is no longer allowed to be as it was, with people gathering together below heaven and above hell and being able to communicate with other groups there. Now, as soon as they arrive (which happens right after they die) the evil are kept completely separate, and after a given amount of time in the world of spirits are taken to their places. So the people who have profaned what is holy—the ones who claimed for themselves the power to open and close heaven and to forgive sins (a power that actually belongs to the Lord alone), the ones who made the pope's proclamations equal to the Word and had power over others as their primary goal—from now on these individuals are taken straight to the black ocean or into the chasms where the hells of the profaners are.

I have been told by a heavenly source that the individuals of this religion who are like this pay no attention to life after death, because at heart they deny it. They believe only in life in this world. Therefore they care nothing for their plight after death, even though it will wear on to eternity; and in fact, they mock it as a thing utterly inconsequential.

The First Heaven, and How It Was Done Away With

IT says in Revelation, "I saw a great throne and the one who sat on it, from whose face earth and heaven fled away. And no place was found for them" (Revelation 20:11), and later, "I saw a new heaven and a new earth; the first heaven and the first earth had passed away" (Revelation 21:1).

I explained in the first chapter above [§3], and also in what followed, that the new heaven and the new earth and the passing away of the first heaven and the first earth refer not to the heaven we can see and the earth that we live on but to the angelic heaven and the church. In its essence the Word is spiritual and therefore deals with spiritual things; and spiritual things have to do with heaven and the church. In the literal meaning, these are expressed by means of earthly things because earthly things serve as the foundation of spiritual ones; and the Word would not be a divine work if it did not have this kind of foundation, because it would not be complete. The earthly, which is the outermost level of the divine design, brings about completion, so that the inner things, which are heavenly and spiritual, stand firmly on it the way a house stands on its foundation. [2] However, since people have thought about what it says in the Word on the basis of what is earthly rather than what is spiritual, they have understood the heaven and the earth mentioned in these and other passages to mean nothing but the heavens in the physical world and this planet. That is why everyone expects these to disappear and be destroyed, followed by the creation of new ones. So that people will not keep expecting this forever, though, century after century without it occurring, the spiritual meaning of the Word has been revealed to make known the meaning of many things in the Word. These meanings cannot get through to our comprehension as long as we think in purely earthly terms about what is said, and this includes the meaning of the first heaven and the first earth that will pass away.

66 Before I clarify what is meant by the first heaven and the first earth, though, it is important for you to know that the first heaven does not mean the heavens made up of people who became angels from the time of the first creation of this world up to the present, since that heaven is steadfast and will endure forever. In fact, once people have been received by the Lord, they can never be plucked out of his hand.

Rather, the first heaven means a heaven composed of others, of people who had not become angels and in most cases proved unable to become angels. (Just below I will relate who they were and what they were like.) This is the heaven that is said to have passed away.

It is called a heaven because the people in it lived together in high places on rocks and mountains. There they pursued the same kind of pleasures they had enjoyed on earth, but no spiritual pleasures. Many people, as they come into the spiritual world from the physical world, believe they are in heaven when they are in high places, and believe they are experiencing heavenly joy when they experience the kind of pleasures they had enjoyed in this world. That is why the Word referred to it as a heaven, but a first heaven that was going to pass away.

67 It is also important to know that although it is called "the first heaven" it did not include any of the people who had lived in this world before the Lord's Coming. It consisted entirely of people who had lived after his Coming, since (as already explained in §§33–39) there is a Last Judgment at the end of every church. At that time a former heaven is done away with and a new one is created or formed. Between the beginning and the end of a church, allowances are made for all who have lived an outwardly moral life and have maintained reverent and holy outward behavior. This holds true even if they are not doing any of this inwardly, as long as the things they are thinking of inwardly and intending to do can be held in check by the civil and moral laws of society. At the end of a church, though, people's inner natures come to light, and then there is a judgment on those people.

Therefore a Last Judgment has been carried out on the inhabitants of our planet twice before, and a third one has just now happened (see §46 above). Likewise, "heaven" and "earth" have passed away twice before and a new heaven and a new earth have been created—"heaven" and "earth" meaning the church on each level, as noted in §§1–5 above.

We can see, then, that the new heaven and the new earth mentioned in the prophets of the Old Testament are not the new heaven and the new earth mentioned in Revelation. When the Lord was in the world, he brought into being the new heaven and the new earth mentioned by the prophets, and he is now bringing into being the new heaven and the new earth mentioned in Revelation. In the Old Testament prophets, it says of the previous new heaven and new earth, "Behold, I am going to create a new heaven and a new earth, and the former ones will not be remembered" (Isaiah 65:17), and "I will make a new heaven and a new earth" (Isaiah 66:22), not to mention related passages in Daniel.

Since we are now about to deal with the first heaven, which passed away, and since no one knows anything about it, I would like to describe it in the following sequence. **68**

1. Who constituted this first heaven.
2. What it was like.
3. How it passed away.

1. *Who constituted this first heaven.* The first heaven consisted of all the people on whom the Last Judgment was carried out. The Last Judgment was not carried out on people who were in hell or on people who were in heaven or on people who were in the world of spirits (on that world see *Heaven and Hell* 421–520) or on anyone who was still alive in the physical world. The Last Judgment was carried out only on people who had fashioned a sort of heaven for themselves, most of whom lived in the mountains or on rocky heights. These were the people the Lord meant by the goats that he set on his left (Matthew 25:32, 33, and following). Therefore the first heaven consisted not only of Christians but also of Muslims and people of other religions, all of whom had formed heavens like this for themselves in various different places. **69**

[2] I need to say briefly what kind of people these were. They were people who had led lives of outward holiness in the world, but with no concern for inward holiness; people who were fair and honest because of

civil and moral laws but not because of divine laws. So they were external or earthly people, not internal or spiritual people. They were devoted to the church's body of teaching and were even capable of teaching it themselves, but were not living by it. They held positions of responsibility of various different kinds and did useful work, but not for the sake of being useful. Among all the people in the whole world who had lived since the Lord's Coming, these kinds of people and others like them constituted the first heaven. As a result this heaven was very much like the world and the church on earth when these are made up of people who do good not because it is a good thing to do but because they fear legal repercussions and the loss of their reputation, honor, and wealth if they do not do it. People who do what is good for no other reasons than these have a fear of other people, but no fear of God and no conscience.

[3] Most of the Protestants in the first heaven were people who had a belief in salvation by faith alone but no life in accordance with faith, which means caring; they also had a great love of being admired.

The inner natures of all such individuals were closed off when they were in public, so that those natures would not be open to view. However, their inner natures were opened to view when the Last Judgment began; and when that happened it became obvious that they were inwardly obsessed with evils and falsities of all kinds, that they were opposed to the Divine, and that they were actually in hell already. This is because after death each of us is immediately allied with kindred spirits—the good with kindred spirits in heaven and the evil with kindred spirits in hell. However, we do not join them openly until our inner natures have been uncovered. In the meanwhile, we can keep company with people who are outwardly like ourselves.

[4] It is important to know, though, that everyone who was inwardly good and therefore spiritual was separated from them and taken up into heaven, and that everyone who was evil not only inwardly but outwardly was separated from them and cast into hell. This has been going on continually from the moment [the church] began after the Lord's Coming until the moment it ended, when the Last Judgment took place. Only those of the kind described just above remained behind and formed among themselves the communities that constituted the first heaven.

70   There are many reasons why allowances were made for communities or heavens like these. The main one is that through the people's outward holiness, honesty, and fairness they were joined to simple but good-hearted people, whether those people constituted the lowest heaven or were still in the world of spirits and had not yet become part of heaven. This is because in the spiritual world there is a communication among all, and everyone is therefore joined to kindred spirits; and the simple but good-hearted people who live in the lowest heaven and the ones who are in the world of spirits pay attention primarily to outward appearances, although they themselves are not evil people inwardly. So if [those who were joined to them] had been pulled away from them before the appointed time, heaven would have been torn apart at its lowest levels, and yet the lowest level is what the higher heaven rests on as its foundation.

[2] In the following words the Lord teaches that this was why allowances were made right up to the final moment:

> The servants of the owner came and said to him, "Didn't you sow good seed in your field? Where then did these tares come from?" And they said, "Do you want us to go and gather in the tares?" But he said, "No, because in gathering the tares you might also uproot the wheat with them. Let both grow together until the harvest, and at harvest time I will tell the reapers, 'First gather the tares and bind them in bundles for burning; then gather the wheat into the barn.'" The one who sowed good seed is the Son of Humanity; the field is the world; the good seeds are the children of the kingdom; the tares are the children of the evil one; the harvest is the close of the age. As the tares are gathered and burned in the fire, that is how it will be at the close of the age. (Matthew 13:27–30, 37–40)

The close of the age means the final time of the church; the tares mean people who are inwardly evil; the wheat means people who are inwardly good; the gathering and binding of the tares into bundles for burning means the Last Judgment.[a]

---

a. Bundles in the Word mean arrangements within us of truths or else falsities in series, so bundles also mean the people who have such truths or falsities: 4686, 4687, 5339, 5530, 7408, 10303. The Son of Humanity means the Lord as divine truth: 1729, 1733, 2159, 2628, 2803, 2813, 3373, 3704, 7499, 8897, 9807. Children mean desires for truth that arise from doing good: 489, 491, 2623, 3373, 4257, 8649, 9807. Thus the children of the kingdom mean people who love truth because they do what is good, and the children of the evil one mean people who love falsity because they do what is evil. So the latter are called tares and the former are called good seed, because tares mean falsity that comes from evil and good seed means truth that comes from goodness. The seed of the field means the truth that serves goodness, something we receive from the Lord: 1940, 3038, 3310, 3373, 10249. In an opposite sense, seed means falsity that serves evil: 10249. The seed of the field also means nourishment for the mind by divine truth from the Word, and sowing means teaching: 6158, 9272. The close of the age means the final time of the church: 4535, 10622.

[3] In the same chapter, there is much the same meaning in the Lord's parable of the gathering in of fish of every kind; in that story the good fish are put in vessels and the bad fish are thrown away. Then it says, "That is how it will be at the close of the age. The angels will come forth and separate the wicked from among the righteous" (Matthew 13:47, 48, 49). These people are compared to fish because in the spiritual meaning of the Word fish mean people who are earthly and external, whether they are good or evil. On the meaning of the righteous, see the footnote below.[b]

71   2. *What the first heaven was like.* What I said just above can give you an idea of this. Add to that that if people lack spirituality because they have not acknowledged the Divine, have not led good lives, and have not desired truth, but for selfish and worldly reasons have nevertheless taken on the appearance of being spiritual by practicing outward holiness, talking about divine matters, and doing upright things, when they are left to their own devices inwardly, they plunge into the wickedness they have been craving. Nothing holds them back—not fear of God, not faith, not conscience. This is why the moment people in the first heaven were brought into their inner natures, it became obvious that they were joined to the hells.

72   3. *How the first heaven passed away.* This has already been described in dealing with the Last Judgment on Muslims and people of other religions (§§50, 51) and on Catholics (§§61, 62, 63), because these groups too were part of the first heaven. It remains to say something about the Last Judgment on Protestants, also called the Reformed and Evangelicals, or how their part of the first heaven passed away. As already noted [§67], the Last Judgment was carried out only on the people who constituted the first heaven, not on anyone else.

After [the Protestants in the first heaven] had been taken through a process of assessment and brought into their inner natures, they were divided into groups and sorted out either by the evil they loved and the falsity it gave rise to or by the falsity they loved and the evil it gave rise to. Then they were cast into the hells that corresponded to their loves.

---

b. In the spiritual meaning of the Word, fish mean the knowledge that belongs to our earthly or outer self, and therefore also mean people who are earthly or external, whether they are good or evil: 40, 991. Animals of all kinds correspond to characteristics within us: 45, 46, 246, 714, 719, 2179, 2180, 3519, 9280, 10609. The Word refers to people as "righteous" if the Lord's merit and righteousness are attributed to them, but as "unrighteous" if their righteousness and merit come from themselves: 5069, 9263, 9486.

Their hells were on all sides of the central area, because, as shown above in §48, Protestants were in the middle, with Catholics around them, then Muslims around them, and finally people of other religions on the outside. Those among them who were not cast into hells were sent away into wilderness areas. Some of them, though, were sent off into plains to form communities in the southern and northern regions, where they would be taught and prepared for heaven. These are the ones who were saved.

As for the details of how all this happened, though, they cannot be described here. The Protestant judgment lasted a long time and was carried out gradually, in stages; and because I saw and heard during that time many things worth mentioning, I would like to present them in sequence as part of the explanation of the Book of Revelation.

The State of the World and the Church from Now On

THE state of the world from now on will be very much the same as it has been up to the present. This is because the immense change that has taken place in the spiritual world does not impose any change on the earthly world with respect to its outward form. So the business of civil life will go on afterward as it did before; there will be times of peace, and treaties, and wars as there were before; and other things characteristic of communities on both a large and a small scale will continue.

When the Lord said that in the last times there will be wars, that nation will then rise against nation and kingdom against kingdom, and that there will be famines, plagues, and earthquakes in various places (Matthew 24:6, 7), he was referring not to events like this in the earthly world but to events in the spiritual world that correspond to such events on earth. The prophecies in the Word are not about kingdoms on earth or nations here, so they are not about wars between them. They are not about famines, plagues, or earthquakes on earth either, but about events that correspond to all these in the spiritual world. In *Secrets of Heaven* there are explanations of what these events are like: for references, see the footnote below.[a]

[2] As for the state of the church, though, this is what will not be the same from now on. It will be similar in outward appearance, but different with respect to what lies within. Outwardly, the churches will continue to be divided as they have been, each will continue to put forward its own body of teaching as it has in the past, and the religions among non-Christians will continue to be much the same as they have been. However, from now on the people in the church will have greater freedom of thought concerning matters of faith and concerning spiritual things that have to do with heaven because their spiritual freedom has been restored. Everything in the heavens and the hells has now been brought back into its proper order, and it is either from the heavens or from the hells that all our thinking in favor of divine principles or against them flows in—our thinking in favor of divine principles flows in from the heavens and our thinking against them flows in from the hells. We do not notice this inner change of state, though, because we do not reflect on it or know anything about spiritual freedom or about inflow. It is perceived in heaven, though, and after we die we will perceive it too.

It is because spiritual freedom has been restored to us that now the spiritual meaning of the Word has been disclosed and its inner divine truths unveiled. In our former state we would not have understood the spiritual meaning, and anyone who did understand it would have profaned it.

On the fact that we have freedom by means of the balance between heaven and hell and that we can be reformed only while in a state of freedom, see *Heaven and Hell* 597–end.

74 I have had various conversations with angels about the future state of the church. They said that they do not know what is to come, because

---

a. Wars in the Word mean spiritual battles: 1659, 1664, 8295, 10455. Therefore all weapons of war mentioned in it, such as bows, swords, and shields, mean weapons used in spiritual battles: 1788, 2686. Kingdoms in the Word mean churches and their truths and falsities: 1672, 2547. Nations mean people who are focused on doing good or else people who are focused on doing evil: 1159, 1205, 1258, 1260, 1416, 1849, 4574, 6005, 6306, 6858, 8054, 8317, 9320, 9327. Famine means a lack of knowledge about what is good and true (1460, 3364, 5277, 5279, 5281, 5300, 5360, 5376, 5893); it also means a desolate state in the church (5279, 5415, 5576, 6110, 6144, 7102). A plague means the stripping away and annihilating of what is good and true: 7102, 7505, 7511. An earthquake means a fundamental change in the state of the church: 3355.

knowing the future belongs to the Lord alone. They do know, though, that the inner slavery and captivity that the people in the church have suffered until now has been taken away; and that now, because freedom has been restored, people can have a better perception of inner truths if they choose to and in this way can become people of greater depth if they wish. However, the angels said they have only slight hope for people of the Christian church along these lines, but more hope for a particular group of people distant from the Christian world and beyond the reach of its proselytizers. The nature of these people is that they are capable of receiving spiritual light and becoming heavenly, spiritual individuals. The angels added that inner divine truths are being revealed to these people at the present day and are being accepted with a spiritual faith—that is, in their lives and in their hearts—and that these people lovingly worship the Lord.

THE END

Supplements

on
the Last Judgment
and
the Spiritual World

Supplement on the Last Judgment

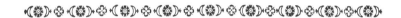

The Last Judgment Has Taken Place

THE earlier booklet *Last Judgment* dealt with the following subjects:

2   The primary purpose of this supplement to *Last Judgment* is to make known what the state of the world and the church was like before the Last Judgment and how that state has changed after it, and also how the Last Judgment was carried out on Protestants.

3   In the Christian world it is commonly thought that on the day of the Last Judgment the whole of the heavens that we see with our eyes and the whole earth that we live on are going to come to an end, that new heavens and a new earth are going to come into being to replace them, and that our souls will then be reunited with our bodies, allowing us to live as human beings again.

This particular belief has arisen because the Word has been understood only in its literal meaning: in fact, there was no other way it could be understood before its spiritual meaning was disclosed. There is also the fact that many people have come to believe that the soul is nothing more than a breath that we exhale and that spirits—and angels, too—are made of wind. As long as that was all there was to their understanding of souls and spirits and angels, there was no other way they could think about the Last Judgment.

In fact, though, we are completely human after death, just as human as we are in this world except that we are then clothed with spiritual bodies rather than our former earthly ones. And spiritual people see spiritual bodies just as earthly people see earthly bodies. Once we come to understand that this is the case, then we are in a position to realize that the Last Judgment is not going to happen in this earthly world but in the spiritual world. After all, that is where all the people who have ever lived and died are gathered together.

4   When we realize this, then we can rid ourselves of absurd notions that would otherwise plague our thinking about the state of our souls after death, about a reunion of those souls with our rotted bodies, about a destruction of the created universe, and therefore about the Last Judgment.

Concerning the state of our souls after death, we would otherwise have the notion that they must be like a breath or a breeze or like ether, fluttering around in the air or else being no longer in space at all but instead in that "somewhere-or-other." We will not be able to see anything because souls have no eyes, hear anything because they have no ears, or say anything because they have no mouths—we will be blind, deaf, and mute, and will be in a state of constant waiting, which cannot help but be profoundly depressing—waiting for the day of the Last Judgment when our souls will finally be given back the abilities that were the source of all our life's pleasures. Further, we would think that the soul of everyone from the first creation must be in this wretched state, that people who lived fifty or sixty centuries ago are still fluttering about in the air like this or existing in that "somewhere-or-other," waiting for the judgment. And other depressing things.

Allow me to skip over the absurd notions we would have concerning the destruction of the universe if we did not know that we are just as human after death as before. These notions are all of the same nature, and there are a lot of them. **5**

Once we know that we are not breaths or breezes after death but spirits—and if we have led good lives, angels in heaven—and that spirits and angels have a form that is human in every way, then we can think intelligently about our state after death and about the Last Judgment. We do not need to think about these matters on the basis of an unintelligible faith, a faith that spawns only idle beliefs that are handed down through the ages. We can instead use our intellect to conclude for certain that the Last Judgment foretold in the Word is not going to happen in this earthly world but in the spiritual world, where everyone is gathered together. We can recognize as well that when the Last Judgment happens, that fact will surely be revealed, for the sake of the credibility of the Word.

Set aside for a moment the idea of the soul as a breath that we exhale and think instead about your own state or the state of your friends or your children after death. Don't you think that you are going to live as a person, and don't you think the same of them? And since they would have no life worthy of the name if they had no senses, surely you think they will be seeing and hearing and talking. Think also of how eulogies depict the deceased: they are in heaven with the angels, in white robes, in beautiful gardens. **6**

Now go back to the idea of the soul as a breath that will live without sensations until after the Last Judgment. Couldn't you lose your mind wondering, "What kind of creature will I be? Where will I be all this while? Will I be flying around in the air or left in that 'somewhere-or-other'? But the preacher told me that if I had good beliefs and lived a good life I'd be joining the blessed after I die!"

Believe instead, because it is the truth, that you will be just as human after death as before, the only difference being the difference between what is earthly and what is spiritual. This is what everyone thinks who believes in eternal life and has not been exposed to hypotheses and hearsay about the soul.

7 You can conclude from what has been said so far that the Last Judgment cannot take place in the physical world but can take place in the spiritual world. You can also see that the Last Judgment did in fact happen in that world, from the eyewitness accounts in the earlier booklet *Last Judgment* (§§45–72) and also from the eyewitness accounts of the judgment on Protestants, which follow below [§§14–31].

Anyone who gives it careful consideration might also be able to tell that this has happened from the fact that new information about heaven, the Word, and the church is now being revealed. Who could make all this up out of nothing?

The State of the World and the Church
before and after the Last Judgment

8 WHAT has been said above shows that the Last Judgment has already taken place in the spiritual world; but if there is to be any knowledge about the state of the world and the church before and after that judgment, the following information is essential.

1. What is meant by the first heaven and the first earth that passed away (Revelation 21:1).
2. Who the people of the first heaven and the first earth were and what they were like.
3. Before the Last Judgment on these people was carried out, much of the communication between heaven and earth, and also therefore between the Lord and the church, was blocked.
4. Since the Last Judgment, that communication has been restored.
5. That is why revelations for the new church were given after the Last Judgment and not before.

6. The state of the world and the church before the Last Judgment was
like evening and nighttime; after it, the state is like morning and
daytime.

1. *What is meant by the first heaven and the first earth that passed away,
described in Revelation 21:1.* The first heaven and the first earth in this
passage do not mean the heavens that we here on earth see with our eyes
or the planet that we live on, nor do they mean the first heaven that is
the abode of all the people since creation who have lived rightly. Rather,
they mean gatherings of spirits who made pseudo-heavens for themselves
between heaven and hell; and since all spirits and angels live in lands just
as we do, those lands are meant by the first heaven and the first earth.

I witnessed the passing away of that heaven and that earth; in the booklet *Last Judgment* (§§45–72) I describe what I saw.

2. *Who the people of the first heaven and the first earth were and what
they were like.* This has also been described in the booklet *Last Judgment*
[§§68–71], but since understanding what follows depends on a recognition of who they were and what they were like, I need to say more about
them now.

All those people who gathered below heaven and made pseudo-heavens
for themselves in various places (which they actually called "heavens") were
closely connected with angels of the lowest heaven. The connection, though,
involved only outward matters, not inward ones. Many were "the goats"
mentioned in Matthew 25:41–46 or members of their family. They were
people who had not done evil things in the world and who had lived
good moral lives, but who had not done what was good for good reasons;
they had in fact separated faith from caring and had therefore not regarded
evil deeds as sins. Since they had lived like Christians outwardly, they were
closely connected with the angels of the lowest heaven, who resembled them
outwardly, although not inwardly. These angels were in fact the sheep [men-
tioned in Matthew 25:31–40]. They were people of faith too, but in their
case their faith was the result of their caring.

Because of this close connection, there was no way to avoid making
allowances for the goats, since separating them before the Last Judgment
would have been harmful to the people in the lowest heaven. These people would actually have been dragged down with the others into destruction. This is what the Lord foretold in Matthew:

> Jesus spoke a parable: "The kingdom of heaven is like a man who sowed
> good seed in his field, but while people slept, an enemy of his came and

sowed tares and went away. When the grain had sprouted and bore fruit, the tares also appeared. The servants of the owner came and said to him, 'Lord, didn't you sow good seed in your field? Do you want us to go and gather in the tares?' But he said, 'No, because while gathering in the tares, you might uproot the wheat with them. Let both grow together until the harvest, and at harvest time I will tell the reapers, "First gather the tares and bind them in bundles for burning; then gather the wheat into the barn."' The one who sowed good seed is the Son of Humanity; the field is the world; the good seeds are the children of the kingdom; the tares are the children of the evil one; the harvest is the close of the age. As the tares are gathered and burned, so it will be at the close of the age." (Matthew 13:24–30, 37–40)

The close of the age is the last time of the church; the tares are people who are inwardly evil; the wheat is people who are inwardly good; binding the former in bundles for burning is the Last Judgment on them; "because while gathering in the tares, you might uproot the wheat with them. Let both grow until the harvest" means that by separating them before the Last Judgment harm might have been done to good people.

11   3. *Before the Last Judgment on these people was carried out, much of the communication between heaven and earth, and therefore between the Lord and the church, was blocked.* Any enlightenment we have comes to us from the Lord through heaven and enters us by an inner route. As long as there were gatherings of people like this between heaven and the world, that is, between the Lord and the church, we could not be enlightened. It was like what happens when the brilliance of the sun is obscured by the interference of a black cloud or when the sun is eclipsed by the moon and its light is cut off. This means that if anything had been revealed by the Lord it would not have been understood, or if it were understood it would not have been accepted, or if it were accepted, over time it would have been smothered.

Since all the gatherings that were causing obstructions have now been dispersed by the Last Judgment, we can see that:

4. *Communication has been restored between heaven and the world, that is, between the Lord and the church.*

12   5. *That is why revelations for the new church were given after the Last Judgment had taken place and not before.* This is because once communication is restored by the Last Judgment we can be enlightened and reformed. That is, we can understand the divine truth of the Word, accept it as something we understand, and retain it as something we have accepted. The obstacles have in fact been removed. So John says that after the first heaven and the first earth passed away, he saw a new heaven and a new earth, and then saw the holy city Jerusalem coming down from God out of heaven, prepared as a bride adorned for her husband; and he heard the one who sat on the throne say, "Behold, I am making all things new" (Revelation 21:1, 2, 5).

On Jerusalem as meaning a church, see *Teachings on the Lord* 62–64, and for new principles taught by that church, see §65 there.

6. *The state of the world and the church before the Last Judgment was like evening and nighttime; after it, the state is like morning and daytime.* When the light of truth cannot be seen and truth is not accepted, the state of the church in the world is like evening and nighttime. We can see that this was the state of the church before the Last Judgment from what was said above in §11. When the light of truth becomes visible, though, and truth is accepted, the state of the church in the world is like morning and daytime.

This is why in the Word these two states of the church are called evening and morning or night and day, as in the following passages:

> The holy one said to me, "Until two thousand three hundred evenings and mornings: then the holy place will be set right." (Daniel 8:14)

> The vision of evenings and mornings is the truth. (Daniel 8:26)

> One day that is known to Jehovah will not be day or night, because there will be light around the time of evening. (Zechariah 14:7)

> Someone crying out to me from Seir, "Watchman, what of the night?" The watchman said, "Morning is coming, but so is night." (Isaiah 21:11, 12)

The following sayings of Jesus concern the last time of the church:

> Stay awake, because you do not know when the master of the house is coming—in the evening, at midnight, at the rooster's crow, or in the morning. (Mark 13:35)

> Jesus said, "I must work while it is day. The night is coming, when no one can work." (John 9:4)

For other examples, see also Isaiah 17:14; Jeremiah 6:4, 5; Psalms 30:5; 65:8; 90:6.

Since this is the meaning of evening and morning, in order to fulfill the Word the Lord was entombed in the evening and then rose in the morning.

The Last Judgment on Protestants

14 IN my earlier booklet *Last Judgment,* I dealt with the judgment on the people meant by Babylon [§§53–64] and also gave some information about the judgment on Muslims [§§50–51] and people of other religions. I did not deal with the judgment on Protestants, though. I noted only that they were in the center, arranged there by nationality [§48], with the Catholics around their circumference, the Muslims around the Catholics, and various other non-Christians around the Muslims.

The reason Protestants occupied the center or central area was that they read the Word and worship the Lord. This means that they have the most light; and the spiritual light that radiates from the Lord as the sun (the Lord in essence being divine love) reaches out in all directions and enlightens even the people who are at the outermost circumference, opening them to understand as many truths as their religion can accept.

In its essence, spiritual light is divine wisdom; it enters our understanding to the extent that the knowledge we have gained in the past gives us an ability to perceive it. It does not travel through space like the light of this world but travels through our desire for and perception of what is true, so it comes to the farthest reaches of heaven in an instant. These workings are what give rise to apparent distances in that world.

For more on this subject see *Teachings on Sacred Scripture* 104–113.

15 I need to describe the judgment on Protestants in the following sequence:

1. The Protestants on whom the Last Judgment was carried out
2. The signs and the reckoning that preceded the Last Judgment
3. An outline of what happened during the judgment
4. The salvation of the sheep

1. *The Protestants on whom the Last Judgment was carried out.* The only **16** Protestants on whom the Last Judgment was carried out were individuals who in this world had acknowledged God, read the Word, listened to sermons, observed the sacrament of the Supper, and had not neglected the church's holy days of worship, but who had seen nothing wrong with adultery and various kinds of theft, deceit, vengefulness, hatred, and the like. Even though they acknowledged God, they thought nothing of sins against him; they read the Word but thought nothing of its precepts for life; they heard sermons but paid no attention to them; they took the sacrament of the Supper but did not desist from the evils of their prior life; they observed the holy days of worship, but did nothing to amend their lives. So outwardly they lived as though they were religious, but inwardly they had no religion whatsoever.

[2] These were the people meant by the dragon in Revelation 12, for it says there that the dragon appeared in heaven, fought with Michael in heaven, and drew down a third of the stars of heaven. It says these things because people like this communicated with heaven by virtue of their acknowledgment of God, their reading of the Word, and their outward worship.

They are also meant by the goats in Matthew 25:[41–46], who are not told that they have done evil things but that they have failed to do good things. All such people fail to do good things that are genuinely good, because they do not turn their backs on evil deeds as sinful; even though they do not do them, they see nothing wrong with them. This means that they are doing them in spirit, and even do them physically when they can get away with it.

The Last Judgment was carried out on all these Protestants. It did **17** not involve Protestants who had no belief in God, felt contempt for the Word, and threw the holy principles of the church out of their hearts, since all such Protestants had been cast into hell when they came from the earthly world into the spiritual world.

All the people who had lived like Christians outwardly and yet saw **18** no intrinsic value in living a Christian life made common cause with the heavens outwardly but with the hells inwardly. Since their connection with heaven could not be abruptly cut off, they were kept in the world of spirits, which is halfway between heaven and hell, and were allowed to form communities there and to live together just as they had in this world. They were also allowed to use arts unknown in our world to make everything look wonderful there and so to convince themselves and others that they were indeed in heaven; so on the basis of these appearances they called their communities "heavens." These "heavens" and "earths" where they lived are the ones meant in Revelation 21:1 by the first heaven and the first earth that passed away.

19 As long as they stayed there, the deeper levels of their minds were closed and the outward levels were open, so the evils that united them to the hells did not show. Once the Last Judgment started, though, their deeper levels were revealed; and then everyone could see what they were really like. Since they were in full cooperation with the hells, they could no longer pretend to live a Christian life but instead rushed enthusiastically into all kinds of evil and wicked practices. They turned into devils and even looked like devils—some black, some fiery, some as gray as corpses. The ones who were full of pride in their own intelligence looked black; the ones obsessed with gaining power over everyone looked fiery; and the ones who totally disregarded and had contempt for the truth looked as gray as corpses.

That is how the scenes of their drama changed.

20 In the world of spirits, which is halfway between heaven and hell, Protestants make up the core, or form a central area, and are arranged there by nationality. In that central area, the British are in the middle, the Dutch to the south and east, the Germans to the north, the Swedes to the west and north, and the Danes to the west; but of these nationalities, only those people live in that central area whose earthly lives were governed by caring and by the faith that comes from caring. There are many communities there. Around them are Protestants who did not lead lives of faith and caring. These are the ones who made pseudo-heavens for themselves.

Heaven, though, is arranged differently than this, and so is hell.

The reason Protestants occupy the central area there is that the Word is read among them and the Lord is worshiped as well, which means that this is where the greatest light is—a light that spreads from there as from its center to the whole circumference, and brings enlightenment. The light in which spirits and angels live comes from the Lord as the sun. That sun, in its essence, is divine love, and the light that radiates from it is, in its essence, divine wisdom. This is the source of everything spiritual in that world.

On the Lord as the sun in the spiritual world, and on the light and warmth that come from it, see *Heaven and Hell* 116–140.

The whole arrangement of communities in that world is an arrange- **21** ment based on differences among various kinds of love. This is because love is our very life; and the Lord, who is divine love itself, arranges these differences according to the way that that love is received. Further, the various kinds of love are beyond counting and are known to the Lord alone.

The Lord joins the communities together in such a way that they all, in effect, lead one human life—the communities of the heavens leading one life of heavenly and spiritual love, and the communities of the hells, one life of demonic and hellish love. He also joins the heavens and the hells in mutual opposition.

Because there is this kind of arrangement, after death we all go to the community of our own love. We cannot go anywhere else, because our love strongly resists our doing so.

This is why people who are devoted to spiritual love are in heaven and people who are devoted only to earthly love are in hell. Spiritual love is given us solely through a life of caring. If we neglect a life of caring, our earthly love remains earthly; and earthly love that is not subservient to spiritual love actually opposes it.

With this in mind we can tell which Protestants were subject to the **22** judgment. It was not the ones who were in the central area but those around them, who, as noted, seemed to be Christians because of their outward morality but who were not Christians inwardly, because they had no spiritual life.

2. *The signs and the reckoning that preceded the Last Judgment.* Above **23** the people who had made pseudo-heavens for themselves something like storm clouds appeared as a result of the Lord's presence in the angelic heavens that were overhead, especially his presence in the lowest heaven. His presence increased there in order to prevent any of that heaven's inhabitants from being carried off to destruction at the same time because of the closeness of their connection [with the pseudo-heavens].

The higher heavens also came down closer to them, which revealed the deeper levels of the people on whom the judgment was about to come. Once this happened these people no longer bore any resemblance to moral Christians as they had before, but became instead like demons. They rioted and squabbled with each other about God, the Lord, the Word, faith, and the church; and since their compulsions to evil had been given free rein as well, they rejected all these things with contempt and ridicule, and plunged into wickedness of every kind.

That is how the state of these supposed heaven-dwellers changed.

At the same time, all the wonderful things they had made for themselves by arts unknown in the world vanished. Their mansions turned into wretched huts, their gardens into swamps, their churches into rubble, and even the hills they lived on into piles of rocks and other such things that corresponded to their lawless dispositions and compulsions. This is because everything we see in the spiritual world corresponds to the feelings that are prevalent among spirits and angels.

These were *signs* of the coming judgment.

24 As the revealing of their deeper natures increased, the hierarchy among these inhabitants changed and was reversed. The ones who made the strongest arguments against the holy principles of the church invaded the center and took control, while the rest, whose arguments were less forceful, retreated to the circumference and hailed the ones in the middle as their guardian angels.

In this way they bound themselves into bundles for hell.

25 In connection with these changes of their state, there were various disturbances of the dwellings and lands around them, followed by earthquakes, which were massive because their [spiritual] upheavals were massive. Here and there, too, gaps opened up toward the hells that were underneath them, and in this way communication with those hells was opened. Then I could see great exhalations that looked like smoke with sparks of fire rising up.

These were also signs that came in advance. They were the ones meant by what the Lord said in the Gospels about the close of the age and then the Last Judgment:

> Nation will rise against nation. There will be great earthquakes in various places. There will be fearful sights and great signs from heaven. And there will be distress of nations, the sea and the waves roaring. [Luke 21:10, 11, 25]

26 *The reckoning* was carried out by angels. Before any community that is bound together by evil comes to an end, there is always a reckoning first. During the reckoning the angels kept urging the people to change their ways and threatening them with destruction if they did not.

During that time the angels also explored whether there were any good people among them, and removed these from the community; but the crowds were so stirred up by their leaders that they hurled insults at the angels and charged at them, trying to drag them into the public square and torment them in all kinds of unspeakable ways. What happened there was like what happened in Sodom.

Many of them came from a faith separated from caring; and there were a few as well who claimed to believe that caring was important but still lived wicked lives.

3. *An outline of what happened during the judgment.* The reckoning and the signs foretelling the coming judgment could not make them give up their criminal behavior. Nothing could deter them from their plots to overthrow everyone who acknowledged the Lord as God of heaven and earth, held the Word to be holy, and lived a caring life. As a result, the Last Judgment came upon them; it happened in the following way.

The Lord appeared in a bright cloud, surrounded by angels, and out of the cloud came a sound like trumpets. This was a sign representing the Lord's protection of heaven's angels and his gathering of good people from all sides.

The Lord does not bring destruction on anyone. All he does is protect his own and withdraw them from their communication with the evil. Once the good people have been withdrawn, the evil become fully engaged in their own obsessions and therefore plunge into all kinds of reprehensible behavior.

At that stage all the people who were about to perish gathered together, looking like a great dragon whose tail was stretched out in a curve and raised toward the sky, thrashing back and forth on high as though it wanted to destroy heaven and drag it down. This effort proved fruitless, though, because the tail was thrown back down, and the body of the dragon, which also looked as though it had risen up, sank down again.

I was allowed to see this representation so that I would know, and could make known, which people are meant by the dragon in Revelation. Specifically, the dragon means all those who read the Word, listen to sermons, and observe the rites of the church, but see nothing whatever wrong with the cravings for evil behavior with which they are saturated. Inwardly, they think about acts of theft and cheating, adultery and obscenity, hatred and vengeance, lying and blasphemy, and are therefore living like devils in spirit, although in their outward lives they are like angels. These are the people who made up the body of the dragon. The ones who made up the tail were like these others in regard to their thoughts and intentions, but had been particularly dedicated in the world to faith as something separate from caring.

29 Then I saw what happened to the rocks people were living on: some of them sank to the deepest depths, some were carried far away, some split open in the middle so that the people living on them were cast down into a cave, and some were submerged as if by a flood. I saw the many people on them gathered into groups like bundles, sorted by types and subtypes of evil, and cast far and wide into whirlpools, swamps, marshes, and deserts, all of which were hells.

The rest, who did not live on those rocks but on either side of them (even though they were given to the same kinds of evil), fled thunderstruck to the Catholics, Muslims, and people of other religions and professed those religions. They could do this without even changing their minds because they actually had no religion. To prevent them from leading the others in those religions astray, though, they were driven off and forced down to live with their true companions in the hells.

This provides a general outline of their fate. The details of what I saw are more than can be described here.

30 4. *The salvation of the sheep*. After the Last Judgment was accomplished, joy broke out in heaven and a greater light than ever broke forth in the world of spirits. The nature of the joy in heaven after the dragon was cast down is described in Revelation 12:10, 11, 12. Light broke forth in the world of spirits because those hellish communities had been in the way like clouds that were darkening the earth. A similar light then arose on us in this world, too, bringing us a new enlightenment.

31 Then I saw angelic spirits rising from the lower regions in great numbers and being lifted up into heaven. These were the sheep, individuals from previous centuries who had been held there and protected by the Lord so that they would not be overcome by the malignant aura that flowed out from the dragon and so that their caring would not be suffocated by it.

These are the people meant in the Word by the ones who woke up and came out of their graves, by the souls of those who had been killed because of their testimony for Jesus, and by those who were part of the first resurrection.

Supplement on the Spiritual World

The Spiritual World

THE spiritual world was the topic of the book *Heaven and Hell,* which offers a description of many of the features of that world; and because we all enter that world after death, it also describes what our state will then be like.

32

Surely everyone knows that we will go on living after death, because we are born human, created in the image of God [Genesis 1:27], and because the Lord tells us this in his Word. Until now, though, there has been no knowledge of what life will be like for us then. People believe that we will then be souls, but their concept of a soul is that it is something airy or ethereal, which retains some capacity for thought, but has no eyesight, no hearing, and no ability to speak. Yet the fact is that we are still human beings after death—so much so that we do not realize we are not still in the physical world. As we used to in the world, we see, hear, and talk. As we used to in the world, we walk, run, and sit. As we used to in the world, we eat and drink. As we used to in the world, we sleep and wake up. As we used to in the world, we enjoy making love to our spouse. Briefly put, we are still human in every way.

This makes it clear that our death is simply a continuation of our life. Death is just a transition.

33 There are many reasons for our not knowing that this is the state we will be in after death. One of them is that we have been unable to be enlightened because we have had so little belief in the immortality of the soul. This is clear from the many people, including scholars, who believe that we are the same as animals, our only advantage over them being that we are capable of speech. So even though such people's words affirm life after death, at heart they deny it. This type of thinking has made them so oriented to their physical senses that they cannot believe we continue to be human after death; after all, they do not see [the souls of the dead] with their eyes. So they say, "How can a soul be human?"

It is different for people who believe they are going to go on living after death. Inwardly, they believe that they are going to arrive in heaven, enjoy themselves in the company of angels, see heavenly paradises, stand before the Lord in white garments [Revelation 3:4–5], and so on. No matter how their outer thinking may stray from this when they think about the soul on the basis of scholarly theories, these remain their inner thoughts.

34 It is clear that people are still human after death—even though they are not visible to our physical eyes—from the angels seen by Abraham, Gideon, Daniel, and other prophets; from the angels seen at the Lord's tomb and later from those seen a number of times by John in Revelation; and above all from the Lord himself, who showed the disciples that he was human by being touched and by eating and yet he also vanished from their sight. The reason they could see him was that the eyes of their spirits were opened, and when these are opened we can see things in the spiritual world just as clearly as we see things in this earthly world.

35 Because it has pleased the Lord to open the eyes of my spirit and to keep them open for nineteen years now, I have been granted the opportunity to see what is in the spiritual world and also to describe it.

I swear to you that these things are not mere visions but are things I have seen when I was wide awake.

36 The difference between a person in the earthly world and one in the spiritual world is that the latter is clothed with a spiritual body and the former with an earthly body. A spiritual person sees another spiritual person just as clearly as an earthly person sees another earthly person, but an earthly person cannot see a spiritual one and a spiritual person cannot see an earthly one. This is because of the difference between what is earthly and what is spiritual. (The difference between these could be described, but the description would not be brief.)

On the basis of my own eyewitness experience of many years, I can **37** testify to the following. Just as in the physical world, in the spiritual world there are landmasses, hills and mountains, plains and valleys, springs and rivers, lakes and oceans. There are parks and gardens, groves and forests. There are mansions and houses. There are manuscripts and books. There are jobs and business transactions. There are precious stones, gold, and silver. To put it briefly, that world contains absolutely everything that exists in the physical world, although in heaven, these things are infinitely more perfect.

In general, the difference is this. Everything in the spiritual world **38** comes from a spiritual source and is therefore spiritual in its essence. The source of everything there is a sun that is pure love. Everything in this earthly world comes from an earthly source and is therefore earthly in its essence. The source of everything here is a sun that is pure fire.

As a result, spiritual people need to be nourished by food that is spiritual in origin, just as earthly people need to be nourished by food that is earthly in origin.

There is more on this topic in *Heaven and Hell* [§§111, 116–125, 340, 582].

The British in the Spiritual World

WE have two levels of thought, outer and inner. In our outer think- **39** ing we are in this earthly world, but in our inner thinking we are in the spiritual world. In good people these levels are in harmony with each other, but in evil people they are not. In this earthly world it is rarely clear what someone is like inwardly, because from early childhood we have tried to be moral and have learned to seem so; but in the spiritual world our nature is plain to see. Spiritual light uncovers this. And we are then spirits, and the spirit *is* the inner self.

Since I have been granted the opportunity to be in that light and to see by that light what the inner selves of people from various nations are like—this through associating with angels and spirits for many years—I have a duty to reveal this information; it is important.

I will first say something about that excellent nation, the British.

40 The better individuals among the British people are at the center of all Christians (see §20 above on the Christians being at the center [of the world of spirits]). This is because they have a profound intellectual light. This trait of theirs is not noticeable to anyone in the earthly world but it is obvious in the spiritual world. They owe this light to their freedom of thought and consequent freedom of speech and writing. (Among other peoples who have no such freedoms, the intellectual light is smothered because it has no outlet.)

This light is not automatically activated in them, however; it is stimulated by others, especially by those who are famous or powerful among them. As soon as people hear statements from these authorities or read something they have recommended, then this light blazes forth; it rarely happens before [such stimulation].

Because of this the British in the spiritual world are assigned governors and are given preachers renowned for their scholarship and brilliance. The people willingly obey edicts and advice from them because to do so is in their nature.

41 They seldom leave their own community in the spiritual world because they love it the way they loved their country in the physical world. They all have similar dispositions, too, which lead them to associate closely with friends from their own country, and rarely with others. They also help each other out and love honesty.

42 There are actually two major cities just like London in the spiritual world. Most British people come into one or the other of them after they die. I have been granted the opportunity to see these and to walk around in them.

The center of one of them is [like] the part of London, England, where the merchants are concentrated, which is called the Exchange. That is where their governors live. Above that city center is the eastern quarter; below it is the western quarter; on its right side is the southern quarter, and on its left is the northern quarter.

[2] In the eastern quarter reside individuals who were more devoted than others to leading a life of caring. The mansions there are magnificent. The wise live in the southern quarter; they have an abundance of glorious possessions. In the northern quarter live people who more than others had loved freedom of speech and of writing. In the western quarter

live individuals who profess faith [alone]. There is an entrance to the city toward the right in this last area, and there is also an exit from the city there. Individuals who live evil lives are sent away through that exit.

The priests who live in the west—who, as just noted, profess faith [alone]—do not dare come into the city [center] by its main streets, but enter instead by rather narrow alleys, because no one is allowed to live in the city [proper] except those who are devoted to a faith that comes from caring.

[3] I have heard complaints raised about the preachers from the west—that they compose their sermons with such skill and eloquence, weaving in a concept of justification by faith that is foreign to their listeners, that the listeners cannot tell whether one is supposed to do what is good or not. They preach a goodness within that they distinguish from outer goodness, sometimes calling the latter "credit-seeking" and therefore unacceptable to God—though they still call it good because it is useful. However, when people from the eastern and southern quarters of the city hear sermons on these mystical topics they walk out of the building; and later those preachers are stripped of their priesthood.

The other major city that is like London is not in the Christian central area described in §20 but lies outside it, to the north. British people who have been inwardly evil come into this London after they die. In the center of it there is open access to hell. Hell swallows these people up from time to time.   **43**

I once heard some priests from Britain talking to each other about faith alone and saw a kind of statue they had made to represent how they saw faith alone. In the dim light they had, it looked like a huge giant, and to their eyes it had a beautiful human form; but when light from heaven was let in, the upper part looked like a monster and the lower like a serpent, not unlike the description of the Philistines' idol, Dagon [Judges 16:23; 1 Samuel 5]. When they saw this, they backed away, and some bystanders threw the statue into a pond.   **44**

From people from Britain in the spiritual world I have gathered that they have two different religious perspectives: one is focused on teachings about faith, and the other on teachings about the way to live. Individuals who have been ordained into the priesthood are focused on teachings about faith, while individuals who have not been ordained (commonly known as the laity) are focused on teachings about how to live. This focus on how to live is manifestly present in the prayer read in churches on Sundays to people who are about to take the Holy Supper, in which   **45** it is clearly stated that if they are not turning their backs on evil deeds because they are sins, they are casting themselves into eternal damnation, and that if they come to take Holy Communion on any other terms, the Devil will enter into them as he entered into Judas [Luke 22:3; John 13:27].

I have occasionally talked with British clergy about the discrepancy between this teaching of the importance of how we live and the teachings about faith. They gave no response, but were having thoughts that they did not dare express.

You may find this prayer in §§5, 6, and 7 of *Teachings about Life for the New Jerusalem.*

46 I have often seen a particular British man who became famous because of a book he had published some years before, a book in which he labored to prove a union of faith and caring through the inflow and inner working of the Holy Spirit, proposing that this inflow affects us in an indescribable way and without our awareness of it. However, it does not touch, let alone move, our will or arouse our thinking to do anything in apparent independence, except by simply allowing actions to happen, first because no aspect of ourselves should enter upon and mingle with divine providence, and also because evil should not in this way affront God. This rules out outward works of caring as being of any benefit to our salvation but nevertheless advocates them for the public good. Because his arguments were ingenious and no one saw the snake in the grass, this book was accepted as the height of orthodoxy.

[2] After his departure from the world this author held to the same dogma and was unable to retreat from it because he had thoroughly convinced himself. Some angels talked with him and told him that his dogma was not the truth but only an eloquent presentation of something clever, and that the truth was that we should abstain from doing evil and do good as though we were doing it on our own, but with a recognition that it was being done by the Lord. They said that until we do that, there is no faith at all, and certainly not the complex thing that he was imagining and calling "faith." Since this conflicted with his dogma, he was encouraged to use his astute intellect to inquire further and see whether this kind of unrecognized inflow and inner working actually did occur, without any outward effort on the individual's part. He seemed then to focus his mind and to follow wandering paths in his thought, always with the conviction that this was the only way we could be restored to wholeness and be saved. Every time he reached the end of a path, though, his eyes

were opened and he saw that he had gone astray. He actually admitted it to some who were present.

[3] For a couple of years I saw him wandering like this; and at the end of his journey, he admitted that there was no such inflow unless the evil in the outer self was removed, which was accomplished by turning one's back on evil because it is sinful, in apparent autonomy. Eventually I heard him say that all the people who convinced themselves of this heresy had been driven insane by their pride in their own intelligence.

I talked with *Melanchthon* and asked him about his situation. He did not want to answer, so I was told about his situation by others. They said that he was sometimes in a stone-vaulted room and sometimes in hell, and that because it was so cold in the room, he seemed to be wearing a bearskin. They said that because of the uncleanness of his room he did not admit newcomers from the world who came to him as visitors, drawn by his reputation and fame.   **47**

He still talked about faith alone, something he had done more to establish than anyone else in the world.

The Dutch in the Spiritual World

I stated in §20 above that Christians among whom the Word is read and the Lord is worshiped are at the center of the nations and peoples of the whole world of spirits because they are in the greatest spiritual light; and the light radiates from them as from a center into the entire surroundings, even the most remote, and brings enlightenment (see what is presented in *Teachings for the New Jerusalem on Sacred Scripture* 104–113).   **48**

Within this Christian central region, Protestants are assigned particular places according to how receptive they are to spiritual light from the Lord. Since the British have that light hidden away in the intellectual part of themselves, they are in the inmost region of that central area. The Dutch, though, keep that spiritual light more closely connected to earthly light, which means that the light they see is not as snowy white. Instead, they see something that is not completely clear, but is receptive to a rationality that comes from both spiritual light and spiritual warmth; so they have been given homes in the eastern and southern parts of that central Christian area. They have homes in the east because they are receptive to spiritual warmth, which is their caring, and homes in the south because they are receptive to spiritual light, which is their faith.

[2] See *Heaven and Hell* 141–153 on these facts: that geographical regions in the spiritual world are not like geographical regions in the earthly world; that the particular region people live in depends on how receptive they are to faith and love; and that the people in the east are the ones who excel in love and caring, while the people in the south are the ones who excel in intelligence and faith.

[3] Another reason they are in the central area of the Christian region is that for them, business is what they love most and money is loved as a means; and this is a spiritual love; but when money is what is loved most and business is loved as a means, that is an earthly love that comes from greed.

The Dutch are more devoted than anyone else to the spiritual love just mentioned. That love truly equates to the common good, and this includes and subsumes the good of the nation.

49 The Dutch hold more firmly to their religious principles than others do. They will not be moved. If someone proves to them that this or that teaching is out of step with the other things they believe, they still will not accept it. They turn away and remain fixed in the position they had held before. They also avoid undertaking any investigation of inner truth; on spiritual matters they keep their rational faculty strictly obedient [to what they already believe].

Since this is their nature, when they come into the world of spirits after death they are brought to accept spiritual teachings from heaven, which are divine truths, in a completely different way than others are. They are not taught them, since they are not receptive. Instead, this is what they go through: They are offered descriptions of what heaven is like, and then are granted the opportunity to go up to heaven and see it for themselves. Then anything [there] that is in harmony with their own disposition is instilled into them and they are brought back down to their own people, full of a longing for heaven.

[2] For example, suppose that they do not accept the truth that God is one in person and in essence, that that God is the Lord, and that the Trinity is within him. Suppose, too, that they do not accept the truth

that faith and caring, even if they are acknowledged and made the subject of conversation, do not accomplish anything unless people actually live them, and that faith and caring are given by the Lord when we turn our backs on evil deeds because they are sins. If they do not accept these truths when they are taught them and persist instead in thinking of God as three persons and thinking no more of religious practice than that some such thing exists, they are reduced to misery and deprived of their business until they see that they are completely out of options.

Then they are brought to some people who have everything, whose businesses are flourishing. At the same time, under heaven's influence it occurs to them to think about why these people have this success, and to reflect on what these people believe about the Lord and how they live. They notice in particular that these people turn their backs on evil deeds because they are sins. They even make a few inquiries about it, and what they learn confirms their thinking and reflection.

They then go back and forth, back and forth like this [between their own lives and those of the successful people]. Eventually, they decide of their own accord that if they want to get free of their misery they need to believe and live as these others do. Then they accept this faith and lead this life of caring, and as they do so, they are given wealth and an enjoyable life.

Therefore although they are not open to being corrected by others, in this way the ones who had lived any kind of life of caring in the world can correct themselves and become prepared for heaven.

[3] Thereafter they are more steadfast than other people are, to the point that they could be called embodiments of constancy; they do not allow themselves to be swayed by any faulty rationale, any fallacy, any confusion created by subtly deceptive reasoning, or any misleading insight, no matter how many supporting arguments it might have.

It is easy to identify the Dutch in the spiritual world because they **50** dress as they did in the earthly world, except that the clothes of the ones who have accepted the spiritual faith and way of life just mentioned are neater and more elegant.

The reason they still dress the same is that they remain steadfastly loyal to their religious principles, and in the spiritual world everyone is clothed according to those principles. This is why people in the spiritual world who are devoted to divine truths wear clothes of white linen.

The cities where the Dutch live are protected in a unique way. All **51** their streets are covered and gated to prevent the Dutch from being seen by anyone on the surrounding cliffs and hills. They structure things in this way because of their deep-seated concern to keep their negotiations confidential and not make their intentions public, since in the spiritual world observers can see your plans just by looking at you.

Curious visitors sometimes come there to find out what life is like in those cities. When they are about to leave the Dutch take them to gateways [at the ends] of their streets that are locked, then take them by other routes to more gateways that are locked, until the visitors become thoroughly frustrated, at which point they are finally released. This is done to ensure that they never come back.

[2] Wives who seek to control their husbands live on one side of the city and are allowed to get together [with their husbands] only when the husbands have sent them an invitation, which is done with some formality. Then those couples are taken to homes occupied by married partners, neither of whom is trying to dominate the other. They are shown how well-decorated and clean these homes are and how enjoyable their lives are, and they see that this is because mutual love is part of the couple's marriage. The wives who are attentive to this, and are moved by it, stop trying to control their husbands and instead share life together with them. These couples are then given homes nearer to the center and are called angels.

This is because marriage love is a heavenly love; it has nothing to do with domineering.

53 During the days of the Last Judgment I saw many thousands of people from that nation cast out of those cities and out of the surrounding towns and regions, people who in this world had not performed any good action for the sake of its connection with religion or conscience, but had done so solely for the sake of their own reputation, in order to be regarded as honest so that they could make a profit. When people like this lose their concern for their reputation or profit, which happens in the spiritual world, they plunge into all kinds of criminal behavior, robbing everyone they run into when they are in the fields and outside the cities.

I saw them cast down, some into a burning chasm that extended beneath the eastern quarter and others into a dark cave that extended beneath the southern quarter. I witnessed this on January 9, 1757.

The ones who lived by their religion, though, and had a conscience as a result, were allowed to stay.

54 I have spoken with *Calvin,* but only once. He was in a community of heaven that can be seen toward the front, above the head. He said that he did not agree with Luther and Melanchthon about faith alone, because so often the Word speaks of works and commands us to act, and therefore faith and works are to be united.

I heard from a governor of that community that Calvin was welcome there because he was honest and caused no trouble.

Elsewhere I will discuss what happened to *Luther;* I have seen and heard him a number of times. Here I will say only that he has often tried to let go of his belief about faith alone, but without success, and that therefore he is still in the world of spirits, which is halfway between heaven and hell, and sometimes life is hard for him there.

55

Roman Catholics in the Spiritual World

IN §§53–64 of the booklet *Last Judgment* I wrote about the Roman Catholics and the Last Judgment on them. In the spiritual world Catholics surround the area where the Protestants are, but they are separated from them by an intervening space that they are not allowed to cross. Some from the Order of the Jesuits, though, use devious means to set up channels of communication with Protestants. They also send their agents along uncharted paths with the intent of luring Protestants away from Protestantism. These agents are found out, however, and after they have been punished they are either sent back to their people or cast into hell.

56

After the Last Judgment circumstances in the spiritual world changed. Newly arrived people are no longer allowed to congregate in large groups as they had been doing. Now instead there are pathways assigned for every type of love, whether good or evil. People who arrive from this world immediately take these pathways, which lead them to a community that corresponds to what they love. Evil people are drawn to a community that is closely connected with the hells, and good people to a community that is closely connected with the heavens. This new arrangement prevents people from forming pseudo-heavens the way others did in the past.

57

In the world of spirits, which is halfway between heaven and hell, there are countless communities like this. There are as many communities as there are general and specific kinds of good and evil loves; and in the interim before these communities are either taken up into heaven or cast down into hell, they have a close connection with us in this world, because we too are halfway between heaven and hell.

58 All Catholics who have not been outright idolaters, who have done good things with sincerity of heart because of the teachings of their religion, and who have also focused on the Lord are brought to communities that have been established near the border with the Protestants. There they are given instruction: they hear readings from the Word and sermons about the Lord, and the ones who accept these truths and apply them to their lives are taken up into heaven and become angels.

There are many communities of these kinds of Catholics in each region, and they are thoroughly protected against the cunning, deceitful schemes of monks and against the leaven of Babylon.

All Catholic children as well are in heaven. They have no knowledge of the false teachings of their parents' religion, because they have been raised by angels under the watchful care of the Lord.

59 All people who come into the spiritual world from our earth, including Catholics, are kept at first in the confession of faith and the religion of their homeland. Therefore the Catholics there always have someone set over them to represent the papacy, someone to whom they give the same ritual adoration they gave the pope in the world. It is rare for anyone who has actually been a pope in the world to play the role of pope there. One exception, though, is the person who was pope of Rome twenty years ago. He was given this position in the spiritual world because at heart he had treasured a conviction that the Word was holier than people believed and that the Lord was to be the focus of worship. After he had served as a pope there for a few years, he stepped down and went over to join the Protestant Christians. He is still with them, and is leading a blessed life.

I was granted an opportunity to talk with him. He said that he reveres the Lord alone, because the Lord is God and has power over heaven and earth. He also said that prayers to the saints are of no value and that the same holds true for masses in their honor. He said that in the world he had tried to reform the church but had been unable to for various reasons, which he told me.

When a great northern city where Catholics lived was destroyed on the day of the Last Judgment, I saw him being carried away on a sedan chair and set down in a place of safety. Something quite different happened to his successor.

I may add to this an account of a memorable occurrence. I was granted **60** an opportunity to talk with Louis XIV, the great-grandfather of the present king of France, who during his earthly life had worshiped the Lord, read the Word, and recognized the pope as no more than the head of the church. In the spiritual world he therefore has a highly honored position, governing the best community of people from France.

I saw him once apparently going down a flight of stairs, and after he had done so I heard him say that it seemed to him as though he were at Versailles. Then there was silence for a couple of hours, after which he said that he had just talked with his great-grandson, the king of France, about the Bull *Unigenitus,* saying that he himself no longer held his former position on it; he now did not accept the bull, because it was detrimental to the French nation. He said that he had impressed this thought very deeply upon the current king's mind.

This happened at about 8 P.M. on December 13, 1759.

The Catholic Saints in the Spiritual World

IT is common knowledge that we all have innate, that is, inherited, evil **61** from our parents, but few know what that evil is. It consists of a love of controlling others. The nature of this love is that the more its reins are let out, the more it breaks forth until it becomes a burning desire to control everyone; ultimately it wants to be called upon and worshiped as God.

This love is the serpent that deceived Eve and Adam. It said to the woman, "God knows that on the day when you eat of the fruit of the tree your eyes will be opened, *and then you will be like God*" (Genesis 3:4, 5). The more the reins are let out, then, and we plunge into this love, the more we turn away from God and toward ourselves and become atheists. Then the divine truths of the Word may indeed serve us as means; but since our goal is to have control over others, we take the means to heart only to the extent that is expedient for us.

This is why the people who have this love of controlling others, whether at an extreme level or only halfway, are all in hell. In fact, this demonic love is present wherever you encounter people who by nature cannot stand even a mention of God.

62 This love is characteristic of those Catholics who exerted control over others because of the irresistible itch of the pleasure involved, and who had no use for the Word and preferred the decrees of the pope. First they are deprived of all their outer knowledge so completely that they no longer know anything about the church; then they are cast into hell and become devils.

There is a particular separate hell for the ones who want to be called upon as gods. The people who live there are so deep in fantasy that they see not what is, but what is not. It is like the delirium of people with a severe fever who see little things in the air, in the room, and on their bedspread that are not there at all.

This worst of all evils is meant by the head of the serpent that was trampled by the seed of the woman, and that wounded his heel (Genesis 3:15). The heel of the Lord (who is the seed of the woman) is the emanating divine influence at the outermost level, which is the Word in its literal meaning.

63 Given the fact that we inherit this characteristic of wanting control [over some people]—and gradually, as the reins are let out, wanting control over more people and eventually over everyone—and since at its core this love is a desire to be called upon and worshiped as God, therefore all the people who have been canonized by papal bull are moved out of sight of others and hidden away, cut off from any contact with those who worship them. This is to prevent that worst root of their inner evils from being activated, which would lead them into the delirious fantasies of the hell mentioned just above. This kind of delirium obsesses people who during their earthly lives longed and worked to become saints after death so that people would pray to them.

64 When arriving in the spiritual world, many Catholics, particularly the monks, look for their saints, especially the patron saint of their order. They are bewildered when they cannot find them. Later, others inform them that their saints are living as ordinary people, among either those in the heavens or those in the hells, depending on how they lived their life in the world; and in either case they are completely unaware that anyone is worshiping them or praying to them. (The ones who do know and who want to be prayed to are in that separate, delusional hell mentioned just above.)

The worship of saints is so distasteful in heaven that as soon as such worship is mentioned the angels shudder, because to the extent that worship is offered to any human, worship is diverted from the Lord. In this case, he is not the sole focus of worship, and if the Lord is not our sole focus, there is a division that robs us of our relationship with him and the happiness of life that flows from it.

To teach me what the Catholic saints are like so that I could make 65 the information known, a hundred or so of them who knew they had been canonized were brought up from the lower earth. Most of them rose up behind me—only a few in front of me.

I talked with one who was said to have been Xavier. When he was talking with me he was behaving very foolishly. He did manage to tell me, though, that when he remained where he belonged he was not a fool, but became one whenever he thought of himself as a saint.

I heard a murmur to the same effect from the ones who were behind me.

It is different for the so-called saints who are in heaven. They know 66 nothing whatever about what is happening on earth; and when I talked with them, no such idea ever came to their minds.

On just one occasion, Mary, the Lord's mother, passed by. I saw her overhead, dressed in white. She paused for a moment and said that she had been the Lord's mother and that he had indeed been born of her, but that when he became God he shed everything human that he had received from her. Now, therefore, she reveres him as her God and does not want anyone to think of him as her son, because everything in him is divine.

Here I may add another account of a memorable occurrence. To the 67 Parisians who are together in a community in the spiritual world a woman sometimes appears in midair, wearing radiant clothes and having a saintly face. She says that she is Geneviève, but when some begin to worship her, both her face and her clothing change so that she looks like a peasant. She criticizes people for wanting to worship a woman who is no more esteemed among her friends than a servant girl would be, and marvels at the fact that people in the world are taken in by this kind of nonsense.

Some angels said that the reason she appears in that community is to separate worshipers of mere human beings from worshipers of the Lord there.

Muslims and Muhammad in the Spiritual World

68 IN the spiritual world, Muslims appear beyond the Catholics in the west; they form a kind of perimeter around them. The main reason they appear there is that they recognize the Lord as the greatest prophet, a son of God, and the wisest of all, who was sent into the world to teach us.

In the spiritual world, the place where each person lives in relation to the central Christian region, inhabited by Protestants, is determined by that person's acknowledgment of the Lord and of the oneness of God. This is because such acknowledgment joins people's minds to heaven and determines their distance from the east, above which is the Lord. People who lack that acknowledgment in their hearts because they have lived an evil life are in the hells underneath these communities.

69 Since our religion is absolutely central to our nature and everything else about us derives from that center, and since Muslims think of Muhammad whenever they think of their religion, there is always a Muhammad set visibly before Muslims in the spiritual world; and in order to turn their faces toward the east, above which is the Lord, he is placed next to the central Christian region.

This is not, however, Muhammad himself, the writer of the Qur'an, but someone else who plays that role. It is not always the same individual either; it changes. At one time it was a man originally from Saxony who had become a Muslim after being taken captive by some Algerians. Because he had originally been a Christian, he was persuaded to talk to them about the Lord, saying that Jesus was not the son of Joseph, as they had believed in the world, but the son of God himself; he instilled in them a concept of the oneness of the Lord with the Father both in person and in essence.

This Muhammad was followed by others who were persuaded to say similar things, with the result that many Muslims have gained a belief concerning the Lord that could be called truly Christian. These Muslims are brought to a community nearer to the east where they are granted communication with heaven, and eventually are raised into heaven itself.

In the place where this Muhammad is to be found, the fire of a burning torch appears as a sign so that people will know where he is; but this fire is visible only to Muslims.

70 The real Muhammad, the writer of the Qur'an, is not seen in public these days. I was told that in the beginning he was the leader of the

Muslims in the spiritual world, but because he wanted to control all aspects of their religious life as if he himself were God, he was removed from where he was living, which was next to the Catholic region, and was sent down to the right near the southern quarter.

At one point malevolent individuals persuaded several Muslim communities to acknowledge Muhammad as God. To quell this uprising, Muhammad himself was brought up from the lower regions and shown to them. I, too, saw him at that time. He looked like those body-oriented spirits who have no deeper perception, with a face that was almost black. I heard him say only these words: "I am your Muhammad." Shortly afterward he appeared to sink back down and return to his place.

As for their religion, this kind of belief was allowed because it suits the viewpoint of those in the Middle East. That is why it has been accepted in so many nations—this and the fact that in it the rules given in the Ten Commandments are made matters of religious practice, and there is material from the Word in it as well. In particular, the Lord is recognized as a son of God and as the wisest of all. Islam also eliminated the idolatrous practices of many nations. **71**

The reason an inward religion was not opened to them by Muhammad was their polygamy, which causes an unclean atmosphere to blow toward heaven. This is because the marriage of one husband and one wife corresponds to the marriage of the Lord and the church.

Many of them are very receptive to truth and are capable of seeing what is right on the basis of rational argumentation—something I have been able to observe in my conversations with them in the spiritual world. I talked with them about the one God, about resurrection, and also about marriage. **72**

Concerning *the one God,* they said that they see no sense in what Christians say about the Trinity, namely, that there are three persons and that each one is God, and yet they maintain that there is nevertheless one God. I said in response that angels in the Christian heaven do *not* say things like that; they say that God is one person and has one essence, but there is a trinity that exists within him. I added that people on earth refer to this trinity as three "persons," but actually all three exist within the Lord. To support this I read to them the passages in Matthew and Luke about the Lord's conception by God the Father [Matthew 1:18–25; Luke 1:26–38], and then the passage where the Lord says that he and the Father are one [John 10:30]. When they heard this they perceived that it was so and said that the Lord's essence, then, is divine.

[2] As for *resurrection,* they said they see no sense in what Christians say about our state after death. Christians say the soul is something like air or a breeze and is incapable of experiencing any pleasure before being reunited with its body on the day of the Last Judgment. I replied that only a particular group of Christians says things like that; Christians who are not part of that denomination believe instead that they will go to heaven after they die, will talk with angels, and will enjoy heavenly delight, and although they do not specify what that delight is, they see it as being not unlike the pleasures they experience in the world. I added that many things about our state after death are just now being revealed to Christians, things they had not known about before.

[3] I have also had many conversations with them about *marriage,* saying among other things that marriage love is a heavenly love and is possible only between two individuals, and that a husband's partnering with many wives blocks access to the heavenliness of this love. They heard the reasons and perceived the fairness in them. I added that polygamy was permitted them because they were Middle Easterners; if polygamy had not been allowed, they would have been even more vulnerable than Europeans to falling into flagrant adulteries of the filthiest kinds and would have destroyed themselves.

Africans, and People of Other Religions, in the Spiritual World

73 THE people of other religions, who had had no knowledge of the Lord, appear farther from the center than the people who had had such knowledge. They are arranged in such a way that those who are at the farthest edge are all complete idolaters and worshipers of the sun or the moon.

The ones who acknowledge one God, though, and who take precepts like those of the Ten Commandments to be religious principles that determine how they live, are situated in a higher region and therefore have more direct communication with the Christians who are in the central region. Their location keeps this communication from being blocked by Muslims and Catholics.

People of other religions are also sorted by disposition and by their ability to receive light through the heavens from the Lord. Some of them are shallow by nature and some are deep. How deep or shallow they are is attributable not to their native soil but to the religion they practice. The Africans are by nature deeper than the rest.

All the people who acknowledge and worship one God as creator of the universe have a concept of God as a human being. They assert that no one can have any other mental image of God than this. When they hear that many actually think of God as a little cloud, they ask where these people are; and when they are told that they are among the Christians, they say that this cannot be. They are given the reply, though, that these people get this idea from the fact that God is called a spirit in the Word [John 4:24], and they think of a spirit only as a little wisp of cloud, not realizing that every spirit and every angel is a human being. Such people were examined to find out whether the spiritual concept they have now was like the earthly one they used to have, and it turned out that those who inwardly recognize the Lord as the God of heaven and earth have a different spiritual concept than they used to. **74**

I heard a particular Christian elder stating that no one could have a concept of a divine-human being. I saw him taken to various people of other religions, going in sequence to people of greater and greater depth; these people took him to their heavens, and eventually to a Christian heaven. At every step, how they inwardly perceived God was communicated to him; he realized that they all conceived of God as a human being, which is the same as having a concept of a divine-human being.

There are many communities of people of other religions, especially Africans, who, when they have been taught about the Lord through angels, say that it makes perfect sense that God, the creator of the universe, became visible in the material world. After all, he created us and loves us; and how else could he become visible to our eyesight except in human form? When they are told that he did not become momentarily visible the way angels do but was instead born as a human and became visible in this way, they pause for a moment and ask whether he was born of a human father. When they hear that he was conceived by the God of the universe and born of a virgin, they say that this means he has a divine essence, and that **75** because this essence is infinite and is life itself, he was not the same kind of human as others are. Angels then tell them that he looked just like other people do, but that when he was in the world his divine essence, which is intrinsically infinite and is life itself, cast out the finite nature and life he had received from his mother. In this way he took his human nature, which had been conceived and born in the world, and made it divine.

Since Africans think more spiritually within themselves than others do, they understood and accepted this.

76   Because this is also what Africans in this world are like, a revelation is occurring among them at the present time, beginning in central [Africa] and spreading outward, though not all the way to the seacoasts. They acknowledge our Lord as the Lord of heaven and earth. When monks arrive there, the Africans laugh at them. They also laugh at Christians who talk about a threefold Divinity and about being saved by what you think. The Africans say that there are no worshipful people who do not put their religion into practice. If we do not live by our religion, they say, we cannot help but become stupid and evil, because we are not open to anything from heaven. Even malice that is ingenious the Africans call stupid, because within it there is not life but death.

I have heard the angels rejoicing over this revelation [in Africa], since it is opening up for them a communication with the human rational faculty that had previously been closed by a blindness in regard to matters of faith.

I have been informed by a heavenly source that angelic spirits are communicating to the inhabitants of that region what it says in *Teachings for the New Jerusalem on the Lord*, *[Teachings for the New Jerusalem] on the Word*, and *Teachings about Life for the New Jerusalem*, which have just been published.

77   The African men I have talked with in the spiritual world wore garments of striped linen. They told me that these clothes were correspondential, and that the women wore garments of striped silk.

They said of their children that they often ask the women who are their teachers for something to eat, saying that they are hungry, and yet when they are given some food they look at it, taste it to see whether it agrees with them, and eat only a little. Clearly then, the cause is a spiritual hunger, which is a longing for knowing genuine truths. This is an actual correspondence.

When the Africans in the spiritual world are unsure whether something they are perceiving and enjoying is the truth, they draw a sword. If the sword gleams, they know that the truths they are engaged with are genuine; they also know this from the way the sword gleams. This too is caused by a correspondence.

On the subject of marriage, they said that by law they were actually allowed to have more than one wife, but that they still had only one because true marriage love cannot be divided. If it is divided, its essence, which is heavenly, perishes. It becomes superficial and therefore merely lustful. Before long, as its potency dwindles, that love becomes cheapened; and once its potency is completely lost, that love becomes tiresome. True marriage love, on the other hand, which is inward, derives nothing from lust. It lasts forever and grows in potency, and proportionally, in delight.

As for people who come their way from Europe, the Africans said that these are not allowed in. A few, though—most of them monks—do manage to get through. In these cases, the Africans ask them what they know; when the Europeans start speaking about their religious beliefs, the Africans call it nonsense that hurts their ears. They send them off to do work that is useful. If the Europeans refuse to do this work, the Africans sell them as slaves, and by law are allowed to punish them whenever they want. If the Europeans cannot be coerced into doing anything useful, they are eventually sold to social outcasts for next to nothing.

78

Jews in the Spiritual World

BEFORE the Last Judgment the Jews were in a valley on the left side of the central Christian area, but afterward they were transferred to the north and forbidden to interact with Christians unless those Christians were traveling outside of their own cities.

79

In that [northern] region there are two large cities to which Jews are brought after death. Before the Last Judgment both of these were called Jerusalem, but afterward they were renamed, because now that the judgment has taken place "Jerusalem" means the church where the Lord alone is worshiped.

The residents of these cities are governed by converted Jews who caution them not to speak disparagingly of Christ and who punish any who do.

The streets of these cities are ankle-deep in muck and their houses are full of unclean things giving off such foul smells that no one else can come near.

80   From time to time an angel with a rod in his hand appears in midair above them. He leads them to believe that he is Moses. He urges them to give up the folly of waiting for a messiah there, since Christ, who is ruling over them and over everyone, is the Messiah. He tells them that he himself knows this now, and that even when he was living in the world he knew something about Christ. After hearing this they go their way; most of them forget it but a few retain it. The ones who retain it are sent to synagogues of converted Jews, and are taught. The ones who accept this teaching are given new clothes instead of the ragged ones they had been wearing. They are also given a beautifully written copy of the Word and a nicer home in the city.

The ones who do not accept what they are taught are cast down into hells underneath that large region of theirs, many into forests and deserts, where they keep robbing each other.

81   In the spiritual world Jews trade in various commodities, just as they do in this world—especially in precious stones, which they get by clandestine routes from heaven, where precious stones are plentiful.

The reason why they deal in precious stones is that they read the Word in its original language and hold its literal meaning to be holy; and precious stones correspond to the literal meaning of the Word (on this correspondence see *Teachings for the New Jerusalem on Sacred Scripture* 42–45). They sell them to people of other religions who live near them in the northern region.

They also possess the skill to manufacture similar stones and create the illusion that they are genuine, but individuals who do this are severely punished by the governors.

82   More than others, Jews are unaware that they are in the spiritual world; they think they are still in the physical world. This is because they are thoroughly external people and do not think about their religion in an inward way. Therefore they still speak about the Messiah as they had before, saying that he is going to come with David and, gleaming with jewels, go before them and lead them into the land of Canaan, along the way raising up his rod and making the rivers dry so they can cross. The Christians (whom they refer to among themselves as "Gentiles") will then seize the hem of their garments, pleading to be allowed to go with them. They will accept the rich in proportion to their wealth and the rich, too, will serve them. They are unwilling to know that in the Word, the land of Canaan means the church and Jerusalem means the church in respect to its teachings, so

"Jews" means all the people who will be part of the Lord's church. On this meaning of "Jews" in the Word, see *Teachings on Sacred Scripture* 51.

[2] When they are asked whether they truly believe that they are going to come into the land of Canaan, they say that they will indeed go down there when the time comes. When they are told that that land is not big enough for them all, they say that it will be enlarged.

When it is pointed out that they do not know where the Bethlehem [of prophecy] is or who belongs to the lineage of David, they reply that the Messiah who is to come knows this.

When they are asked how the Messiah, the Son of Jehovah, could live among such evil people, they say that they are not evil. When they are reminded that in his song in Deuteronomy 32 Moses describes them and indicates that they are very wicked, they reply that at that point Moses was angry because he was not allowed to go with them; but when they are told that Moses wrote this at Jehovah's command, they fall silent and withdraw to confer.

When they are told that they were originally descended from a Canaanite woman and also from Judah's whoring with his own daughter-in-law (Genesis 38:[2, 16]), they get angry and say that it is enough for them that they are descended from Abraham.

When they are told that there is a spiritual meaning within the Word that is about Christ alone, they say that this is not true; there is nothing within the Word except gold. And more along the same lines.

Quakers in the Spiritual World

THERE are fanatical spirits who are convinced they are divinely inspired. They are kept apart from all others and are so thickheaded that they believe they are the Holy Spirit. When Quakerism was just beginning, these spirits were drawn forth from the surrounding forests where they had been wandering. They infested many individuals [on earth], filling them with the conviction that they were being impelled by the Holy Spirit. And because those who were infested felt an inflow physically, this conviction

83

took possession of them all to such an extent that they believed they were holier and more enlightened than other people. As a result, they could not be induced to give up their [new] religion.

People who have completely convinced themselves of this come after death into the same kind of fanaticism. They are separated from others and sent away to kindred spirits in the forests, where from a distance they look like wild boars. People who have convinced themselves less completely are first separated from others and then sent to a similar place in a wilderness in the far south, where caves serve as their places of worship.

84 After the fanatical spirits just mentioned have been distanced from them and the infestation of quaking that had taken over their bodies has ceased, they then just feel a motion on their left side.

I have been shown that from very early on, Quakers started straying more and more into evil practices, and eventually into heinous acts, under the command of their "holy spirit"—practices they keep secret from everyone. I have talked, though, with the founder of their religion and with Penn, both of whom said that they had had no part in anything like that.

After they die, individuals who have perpetrated such acts are sent away to a place of darkness and they sit in the corners there, looking like the dregs in a bottle of oil.

85 Because Quakers rejected the two sacraments, baptism and the Holy Supper, and yet still read the Word and preach about the Lord, and because when they speak they are possessed by fanatical spirits and therefore mix the holy teachings of the Word with truths that have been profaned, no community is formed from them in the spiritual world. Instead, their associations are broken up and they wander here and there, then disappear from view, and gather in the wilderness location mentioned above [§83].

Moravians in the Spiritual World

86 I have had many conversations with Moravians (also known as Herrnhuters). At first they were to be found in a valley not far from the Jews. After they had undergone examination and had been revealed for what they were, they were taken off to some uninhabited areas.

The examination of them revealed that they were very knowledgeable and skillful in how to captivate people's minds, presenting themselves as a remnant of the apostolic church. For this reason they would call each other "brother" and use the term "mother" of women who were open to learning their deeper mysteries. They also said that they more than others stress faith and that they love the Lord because he suffered on the cross, calling him the Lamb and the Throne of Grace, and more in the same vein, in order to foster a belief that they are the true Christian church. People who are taken in by their smooth words are then examined by the Moravians to see whether they are the kind to whom they would dare disclose their mysteries. If those who are examined are not the right kind, the Moravians keep their mysteries to themselves; but if they find they can disclose their mysteries to them, they do so. They then give them warnings and even utter threats against any of them who would divulge their secret teachings about the Lord.

Since they continued to present themselves in this same manner in the spiritual world, and yet [the angels] perceived that their inward thoughts differed from what they were presenting outwardly, to uncover this discrepancy they were brought into the lowest heaven. They could not stand the atmosphere of caring and consequent faith among the angels there, so they hurried away. **87**

Later, because in the world they had believed that they were the only people who were really alive and that after death they would enter the third heaven, they were actually taken up to that heaven. But when they sensed the atmosphere of love for the Lord there, they felt as though they were having a heart attack. They began to suffer intense inner pain and to have convulsions like people in the throes of death, so they hurled themselves headfirst out of there. This was the first method by which it was revealed that inwardly they attach no value whatever to caring for their neighbor or loving the Lord.

They were then sent to people charged with the task of exploring the deeper levels of their thinking. The report these people made of them was that they despise the Lord, reject the life of caring so completely that they loathe it, regard the Word of the Old Testament as useless, and look down on the Word of the Gospels. All they do with Scripture is take what they please from Paul in the passages where he talks about faith alone. Such are the mysteries that the Moravians keep hidden from the world.

So it became clear that the Lord is someone they regard as Arians do, that the Word of the prophets and of the Gospels is something they **88** despise, and that the life of caring is something they hate, when in fact these are the three pillars on which all heaven rests. Therefore the ones among them who knew and believed in these mysteries were judged to be antichrists who rejected the three essential beliefs of the Christian church—the divine nature of the Lord, the Word, and caring. They were cast out of the Christian world into a wilderness that is at the border of the southern region, near the Quakers.

89   I heard Zinzendorf when he arrived in the spiritual world shortly after his death. He was allowed to talk just as he had previously in the world—arguing that he knew the mysteries of heaven and that no one would enter heaven except those who relied on his teaching. He insisted that those who do good deeds for the sake of salvation are utterly damned, and that he would sooner accept atheists into his congregation than them.

He said that the Lord was adopted by God the Father as his son because of his suffering on the cross, but that he was nevertheless just an ordinary human being. When it was explained to him that the Lord was conceived by God the Father, he replied that he thought whatever he pleased about that but did not dare to talk the way Jews did.

From his followers, too, I sensed multiple objections when I read the Gospels.

90   The Moravians said they had been given a sensation and had taken this as an inner confirmation of their teachings, but they were shown that this sensation had come from delusional spirits who confirm for people whatever constitutes their religion, and that these spirits enter more fully into people who, like the Moravians, are passionate about their religion and are constantly thinking about it. There these spirits actually talked with them, and they recognized each other.

BIOGRAPHICAL NOTE

Biographical Note

EMANUEL SWEDENBORG (1688–1772) was born Emanuel Swedberg (or Svedberg) in Stockholm, Sweden, on January 29, 1688 (Julian calendar). He was the third of the nine children of Jesper Swedberg (1653–1735) and Sara Behm (1666–1696). At the age of eight he lost his mother. After the death of his only older brother ten days later, he became the oldest living son. In 1697 his father married Sara Bergia (1666–1720), who developed great affection for Emanuel and left him a significant inheritance. His father, a Lutheran clergyman, later became a celebrated and controversial bishop, whose diocese included the Swedish churches in Pennsylvania and in London, England.

After studying at the University of Uppsala (1699–1709), Emanuel journeyed to England, the Netherlands, France, and Germany (1710–1715) to study and work with leading scientists in western Europe. Upon his return he apprenticed as an engineer under the brilliant Swedish inventor Christopher Polhem (1661–1751). He gained favor with Sweden's King Charles XII (1682–1718), who gave him a salaried position as an overseer of Sweden's mining industry (1716–1747). Although Emanuel was engaged, he never married.

After the death of Charles XII, Emanuel was ennobled by Queen Ulrika Eleonora (1688–1741), and his last name was changed to Swedenborg (or Svedenborg). This change in status gave him a seat in the Swedish House of Nobles, where he remained an active participant in the Swedish government throughout his life.

A member of the Royal Swedish Academy of Sciences, he devoted himself to studies that culminated in a number of publications, most notably a comprehensive three-volume work on natural philosophy and metallurgy (1734) that brought him recognition across Europe as a scientist. After 1734 he redirected his research and publishing to a study of anatomy in search of the interface between the soul and body, making several significant discoveries in physiology.

From 1743 to 1745 he entered a transitional phase that resulted in a shift of his main focus from science to theology. Throughout the rest of his life he maintained that this shift was brought about by Jesus Christ, who appeared to him, called him to a new mission, and opened his perception to a permanent dual consciousness of this life and the life after death.

He devoted the last decades of his life to studying Scripture and publishing eighteen theological titles that draw on the Bible, reasoning, and his own spiritual experiences. These works present a Christian theology with unique perspectives on the nature of God, the spiritual world, the Bible, the human mind, and the path to salvation.

Swedenborg died in London on March 29, 1772 (Gregorian calendar), at the age of eighty-four.